Center for
Creative Leadership

leadership. learning. life.

Success for the New Global Manager

Maxine Dalton
Chris Ernst
Jennifer Deal
Jean Leslie

Success for the New Global Manager

What You Need to Know to Work Across Distances, Countries, and Cultures

JOSSEY-BASS
A Wiley Company
San Francisco

Center for
Creative Leadership

leadership. learning. life.

Published by

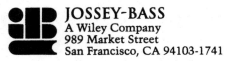

JOSSEY-BASS
A Wiley Company
989 Market Street
San Francisco, CA 94103-1741

www.josseybass.com

Jossey-Bass books and products are available through most bookstores. To contact Jossey-Bass directly, call (888) 378-2537, fax to (800) 605-2665, or visit our website at www.josseybass.com.

Substantial discounts on bulk quantities of Jossey-Bass books are available to corporations, professional associations, and other organizations. For details and discount information, contact the special sales department at Jossey-Bass.

We at Jossey-Bass strive to use the most environmentally sensitive paper stocks available to us. Our publications are printed on acid-free recycled stock whenever possible, and our paper always meets or exceeds minimum GPO and EPA requirements.

Library of Congress Cataloging-in-Publication Data
Success for the new global manager : what you need to know to work across distances, countries, and cultures / by Maxine Dalton
. . . . [et al.].—1st ed.
    p. cm.
"Joint publication of the Jossey-Bass business & management series and the Center for Creative Leadership."
ISBN 978-0-470-63137-9
1. Executive ability. 2. Intercultural communication. 3. International business enterprises—Management. 4. Corporations, American—Management. 5. Success in business. I. Dalton, Maxine A.
HD38.2 .S83 2002
658'.049—dc21   2001008162

FIRST EDITION
HB Printing   10 9 8 7 6 5 4 3 2 1

A Joint Publication of
The Jossey-Bass
Business & Management Series
and
The Center for Creative Leadership

We dedicate this book
to our families and
friends with love
and appreciation.

Contents

Acknowledgments

We wish to recognize the managers from Novartis Pharma, Gate-Gourmet, Motorola University, and Volvo, who graciously agreed to participate in this study, and our internal partners, Gerard Antoine, Frances Coman, Dr. Tracy Elazier, and Ann Hesselbom, who made this partnership possible. We want to especially acknowledge and thank Dr. Walter Ritter and Novartis Pharma for their generous support of this work.

We thank Denise Craig for helping us track down references, permissions, and misplaced clippings and for her general support and assistance. We appreciate the reviews by our internal colleagues—Michael Hoppe, Jennifer Martineau, Jim Penny, Marian Ruderman, and Valerie Sessa—that helped get us to this point. We also thank Zeynep Aycan at KOC University, who reviewed the original project research proposal. We are grateful to Janet de Merode, who assisted with the first literature review, and to Jennifer Maigetter and Gustav Ragettli, who conducted some of the early interviews. And finally we thank the Center for Creative Leadership publications group, especially Marcia Horowitz; Peggy Cartner, CCL's extraordinary reference librarian; and our editors at Jossey-Bass for their support and guidance throughout this process.

About the Authors

Maxine Dalton is group director of the Leading in the Context of Difference practice area at the Center for Creative Leadership (CCL). In this role, she manages research and development projects dedicated to understanding how people become effective managing and leading others who are different from them on some major social dimension. Maxine has managed and trained a program for human resources professionals called "Tools for Developing Successful Executives," and has used 360-degree surveys with groups and individuals in development programs conducted throughout the world. Her list of book chapters, CCL press books, and journal articles on global issues, 360-degree feedback, and human resources issues is extensive, and she also presents and conducts seminars at international colloquia and conferences. She holds a Ph.D. in industrial/organizational psychology from the University of South Florida.

Chris Ernst, a research associate at CCL, focuses on the changing role of leadership in a globally interconnected world. He has significant international experience as a student and a traveler, and prior to coming to CCL, he taught and conducted research for an international business college in northern Spain. Chris has coauthored several articles and frequently presents on global issues. His Ph.D.

in industrial/organizational psychology is from North Carolina State University.

Jennifer Deal is a research scientist at CCL, where she currently heads the Emerging Leaders project. In this role, she investigates the effects of generational issues on leadership. She also has research interests in global leadership, conflict management, mediation, and individual and small-group decision making. Jennifer has authored and coauthored reports and articles on executive selection, global management and development, women in management, and generational issues. She holds a Ph.D. in industrial/organizational psychology from The Ohio State University.

Jean Leslie is manager of Instrument and Development Research at CCL, where she studies the impact of multirater feedback and assessments on individuals, teams, and organizations. In this role, she also designs research programs for CCL instruments and interprets their results. She also is an instructor in the Benchmarks® Certification Workshop and manages the translations of CCL instruments into other languages. Jean has also been active in CCL's work on cross-cultural issues and on derailment and is coauthor of several reports, articles, and book chapters on 360-degree feedback instruments, derailment, and cross-national comparisons. She has an M.A. in sociology from the University of North Carolina at Greensboro.

Success for the New Global Manager

Leaders in the business world should aspire to be true planetary citizens. They have global responsibilities since their decisions affect not just the world of business, but world problems of poverty, national security and the environment.

—A. RODDICK, 1991
Body and Soul
Crown

Introduction

Peter grew up in a rural area of Louisiana and was the first person in his family to graduate from college. He attended a state college and graduated in the top third of his class with a degree in electrical engineering. Had he not worked a series of part-time jobs while in college he might have made even better grades. Peter was offered a job with a major utility company as soon as he graduated, and he accepted it. He progressed steadily from individual contributor to manager because his work was quick and thorough. He soon became manager of the Southeastern region.

Peter has excellent problem-solving and technical skills, and he relishes finding the right answer. He believes that all problems have solutions if one persists long enough. He is respected by his direct reports and peers as a person of integrity and expertise. Peter is focused, pragmatic, smarter than average, achievement oriented, and "linear." That is, he perceives the world as nuts, bolts, screws, and circuit diagrams; he is not drawn to the messy world of human relationships, and doesn't see much use in the notion of leadership development. His interpersonal skills are acceptable, although he tends to be quiet and some people are intimidated by his demeanor. He is not one for small talk, but when he has a question, he asks it. People who know him or who come from a similar orientation and background aren't put off by this behavior. They are somewhat amused. People who don't know him or who come from someplace else tend to perceive him as somewhat rude and unappreciative.

Peter works in Shreveport, Louisiana, and many of his coworkers grew up in the same region or went to the same college. Because he is from the area, Peter has been a successful negotiator and has taken the lead in the past round of negotiations with the union. The union representatives trust him because they know what to expect. He never wastes their time, and he keeps everyone on track. He identifies the problems and solves them.

Peter's organization has recently acquired a French utility company, and Peter has been asked to manage the operation in France that parallels the group in the United States. This job will not require relocation, but it will require him to travel often to Paris and other locations in France in addition to covering his present territory in the United States (Florida, West Virginia, Louisiana, and Pennsylvania). Because Peter has a young family, he hopes to be able to fulfill many of his managerial responsibilities via e-mail, videoconferencing, and teleconference calls, but he is resigned to the probability of spending more time away from home, especially in the beginning.

Peter is ambitious, and he relishes this new opportunity. He knows that because of U.S. deregulation and the role of nuclear energy in the French system that the businesses are not identical, but he is not very concerned about his ability to do this job. After all, he speaks a little bit of French, and he has been on holiday to Paris and the south of France. He is not unfamiliar with the French. In fact, some of his ancestors were French. Peter is, of course, proficient in the use of technology and has worked on many virtual projects. He has already scheduled his first on-line management meeting. He wants to establish a connection with the French company as soon as possible, but at this time he believes he cannot justify a trip merely to "get acquainted."

Peter may not realize it, but his job has just become exponentially more complex. He is now a global manager. He works across seven time zones in two countries on two continents. These two countries have very different cultural values and orientations, as well as very different legal, political, and historical frameworks. Even so, because of Peter's background and past success, you might predict that his next assignment will be a breeze. After all, his new assignment will be the same operation—simply located in France. This assignment represents just another increase in scope, and he's done that before. His responsibilities are magnified but they are not qualitatively different, or are they?

It's a New Scene for Global Managers

Peter might be in for a bit of a shock if he thinks managing globally will be similar to managing in his home country. There will be a number of challenges that he doesn't foresee. He will find business being conducted in ways that will initially strike him as odd. He will discover that what has worked well in the past does not work now at all. And more than likely Peter's image of a global job involves working in different cultures as an expatriate, which is the most familiar model for a manager who works overseas. Expatriates sometimes spend many years traveling and working for an organization in different countries and cultures.

But Peter is not to be an expatriate. He and many others face a much more complex situation in terms of what it means to be a global manager today. He is to become a manager, indeed a coordinator and integrator, of performance results, business acumen, social patterns, and continual technological advances. Global managers are charged with sorting out massive input on various levels and making sense of it for their constituents because they are now in a more *globally complex* environment; that is, they are managing across geographic distance, country infrastructures, and cultural expectations. They face a much broader, more complicated role— one that creates a set of particular leadership challenges.

When Peter begins his new assignment as a global manager, this is what the scope of his job will look like. He will work across multiple time zones, country infrastructures, and cultural expectations. He will not be an expatriate—he will live in the United States and not relocate to France. But every time he tries to do work, he will be dealing with people not from his country. Every time Peter picks up the phone, logs on to e-mail, or steps off an airplane, he will deal with people who may have different sets of cultural expectations. And he will come to understand that these cultural expectations are intrinsic to the laws and customs of the country or region.

We have seen many Peters who are confused about the scope and scale of what global challenges mean in their particular positions. After all, if someone spends his entire career in Shreveport, Louisiana, what does he need to know about managing globally? Plenty, we say. Rarely does a day go by that any manager, in any type of organization, does not come into contact with an individual, policy, or product from another country. Even if individuals don't want to think about it, the choice is becoming increasingly obvious and simple: either learn about global issues or risk getting passed by. How to work effectively with people from other cultures at a distance is a skill every manager must learn.

Nancy Adler stated that the global manager is "concerned with *the interaction of people and ideas among cultures*, rather than the efficacy of particular leadership styles within the leader's home country or with the comparison of leadership approaches among leaders from various countries. . . . Global leadership is neither domestic nor multidomestic, it focuses on cross-cultural interaction rather than on either single-culture descriptions or multicountry comparison" (Adler, 1999, p. 53 [emphasis added]).

In this book we talk about what makes a global manager—that is, one who manages across distance, countries, and cultures—effective in a globally complex environment. We document the scope, scale, and layers of this complexity. We describe global management scenarios that will help you recognize complexity in your own work life and therefore operate more effectively when it occurs.

What is more important, we describe and show you how to identify and develop the *essential managerial capabilities* that are critical to success, whether your work is global or domestic, and give you some tools to analyze your current level of expertise. We will then offer you a set of *pivotal capabilities for global management* that are specifically related to performance in global roles. These skills are what you will need to adapt the capabilities you already have in your current work to globally complex situations. They will enable you to move toward an effective career as a global manager and prevent you from being derailed by the challenges. These pivotal capabilities are not your typical laundry list of required global skills, but rather a specific set of tools that our experience with hundreds of global managers has shown us is essential for effective leadership.

Finally, we will show you how your organization can help you acquire these important capabilities in a globally complex environment.

Why Effective Global Management Skills Are Important

Jack Riechert, past CEO of the Brunswick Corporation, sums it up best: "Financial resources are not the problem. We have the money, products, and position to be a dominant global player. What we lack are the human resources. We just don't have enough people with the needed global leadership capabilities" (Gregersen, Morrison, & Black, 1998). These sentiments have been voiced by a number of executives and top-management teams whose organizations grapple to compete in the global economy. The greatest obstacle to global effectiveness is a shortage of people who are prepared to manage and thrive in this new business paradigm.

Global experience is becoming essential for managers who aspire to the top of an organization. The PricewaterhouseCoopers Annual CEO Survey for 1999 found, "Experience managing multicultural teams is the most valued attribute of a manager, more so than industry knowledge, company experience, or an advanced degree from a top business school. The most sought after managers are the ones who can integrate across cultures, geographies, and disciplines and get the job done." Though this statement was more heartily endorsed by CEOs of European-based companies than by CEOs of companies based in the United States, it demonstrates a growing trend in the United States as well. As globalization has evolved from being the latest business buzzword to a basic economic reality, more and more managers are realizing that global experience is critical to getting the work done.

But most people don't have this experience, and the skills acquired through experience aren't necessarily something that can be taught in a class in business school. For managers who are open and willing to learn, the global economy presents significant new and exciting opportunities.

The Questions We Asked and Why We Asked Them

This book is based on a three-year study with 211 global and local managers working for four major multinationals, two with corporate headquarters in Switzerland and the others in the United States and Sweden. (See Appendix A for a detailed description of the study.) Four kinds of industries are represented in the study—pharmaceuticals, hospitality and service, high-tech manufacturing, and truck and construction manufacturing. The managers were native to thirty-nine countries and during the study were living in thirty countries. All the major cultural regions, taken from the work of Ronen and Shenkar (see Figure 1.1 on page 20), were represented in the study—Latin American, Arab (Middle Eastern), Far Eastern, Latin European, Germanic, Anglo, Nordic, Near Eastern, and independent (countries not easily clustered together)—but the majority of the managers were from the Anglo or Germanic cultural regions.

To help us understand the nature of global managerial work and what it takes to do it well, the managers who took part in our study filled out multiple forms and surveys—each answering nearly a thousand questions in all.

Their responses provided a multidimensional view of each manager that included personality, managerial capabilities, life history, work history, and background characteristics and experiences. In addition to this information, the boss and direct reports of the participating managers provided confidential ratings about managers' performance effectiveness. We compared the results from the *local managers* and their bosses and direct reports with the results from the *global managers* and their bosses and direct reports to provide us with the foundation material for this book. We then combined and integrated what we learned with what others have studied and written.

A New Framework for the Developing Manager

This book is different from most books about globalization and global management and leadership. It is not about the global organization or its structure and strategy; instead, it focuses on individuals who have or aspire to have management responsibilities that are global in scope. It is not based solely on interviews with successful managers at the very top of the organization, though we have done some of that. It is based on a combination of quantitative and qualitative research with managers in a variety of jobs and industries and from varying cultural backgrounds. Some of these managers are effective leaders, and some are not as effective. The book does not simply represent a list of virtues or competencies that the reader should aspire to, but instead provides an integrating and dynamic framework along with direction for acquiring these capabilities. And finally, the book is unique because the capabilities that we describe are indeed related to bosses' and direct reports' performance ratings of managers working around the world.

Organization of the Book

There are two main sections that will help you understand what skills are needed and how you can go about developing those skills. The first section (Chapters One to Three) focuses on what you as a global manager do and what you need to know. The second section (Chapters Four and Five) focuses on helping you learn how to develop the capabilities needed to be successful as a global manager.

In Chapter One we examine the idea that global managers today work in a world that is globally complex. That is, they work across borders of distance, country infrastructures, and cultural expectations. We also present what we mean when we speak of *effectiveness* and provide a list of the questions that the bosses and direct reports in our study used to rate the effectiveness of managers who participated in the study.

In Chapter Two we discuss the capabilities and knowledge that all managers need—what we term the five *essential managerial capabilities*—whether your work is global or domestic in scope. We explain how, though the specific roles and knowledge may be the same, the behaviors needed to fill those roles will be different in different cultures and countries. We also present a set of tools that illustrate how these basic managerial skills must be adapted when they are being used in other cultures and within a variety of legal and political systems.

In Chapter Three we describe the pivotal capabilities for global management in terms of the skills, knowledge, and motivation that you need as a successful global manager to allow you to adapt and change as the situation demands.

Chapter Four presents a dynamic framework for developing the pivotal capabilities. We show you how to integrate who you are, what you already know, and the experiences available to you in order to develop the skills for global management. Given that many organizations are currently limited in their systems for developing global skills, managers must take greater responsibility for their own progress.

Chapter Five is written for the individual manager, but it is also meant for those in organizations who are responsible for the development of others. Here we discuss the dynamics of learning and present a menu of opportunities and experiences that can be used by organizations to select and develop their current and future pool of international managers and executives.

Finally, in the Epilogue we sketch the challenges that we believe represent the next step for global managers: grappling with the ramifications of global business within an even more complex world context.

In each chapter we have included examples and tools to help you gain a more specific understanding of what you already know and what you will need to learn to work in positions that are becoming more globally complex.

Who This Book Is For

We wrote this book for practicing managers and those who work with them (including HRD practitioners) who are responsible for developing either themselves or others for managing in the global economy. Our objective is to help improve managers' capabilities to be effective in a complex, global business environment.

For those of you who are global managers, this will mean improving your effectiveness within your current context. For those who are not working globally but aspire to do so, this will mean knowing what it takes to be effective and taking the necessary steps to get there. And for those who are responsible for the development of others, this will mean using this information to help develop managers who aspire to or are already working in positions that are globally complex.

We expect that for some of you, globalization—like technology—has crept up on you. You may perceive the whole topic as anything from confusing to unsettling to somewhat uninteresting. Having to read international newspapers, learn another language, travel to a foreign country and eat foreign food, and pay close attention to someone speaking English as a second language is not your preferred way of doing business. For others, the larger world is a source of great interest. You want to be more effective globally but may not understand exactly what that means or how to go about getting there. We want this book to take you further down the road toward a way of doing and being that will lead to success in the larger global environment.

In sum, we wrote this book for people who currently hold or aspire to global responsibilities in their organizations. Our hope is that you will come to relish the compelling personal and professional opportunities that will lead to the mastery of managing and leading across distance, countries, and cultures.

PART ONE

The New Global Manager

Today's executives must have a set of capabilities that allow them to successfully manage the complex challenges that attend the global business environment. Through our research and our experience with hundreds of global managers, we have come to understand that you may already use many of these capabilities. We call them *essential managerial capabilities*: ability to manage people, action, and information; ability to cope with pressure; and core business knowledge. These five capabilities are essential to good leadership, whether in a global or local setting. As an effective manager you need to do these things whether working with people in Tucson, Ankara, or both.

We have also identified four *pivotal capabilities*: international business knowledge, cultural adaptability, perspective-taking, and ability to play the role of innovator. The pivotal capabilities are the catalysts you use to adapt and expand on the five essential managerial capabilities when you are managing in an environment of global complexity. You must employ the pivotal capabilities whether you are working simultaneously or one-on-one with your French, Ukrainian, Vietnamese, or Tunisian counterparts across the boundaries of time, country, and culture. But we want to emphasize that the pivotal capabilities are not presented as something for you to just tack on to the essential capabilities. They represent a lever, a catalyst that will help you stretch to meet the demands of global work and fill a gap that has been created, ironically, by advances in technology and communication.

The pivotal capabilities help managers adapt what they already do successfully in their own country to other countries, other cultures, and across multiple time zones. They are the foundation of behaviors and attitudes that effective managers with global responsibilities bring to their work: the ability not only to adapt on a time zone by time zone, country by country, culture by culture basis, but also the ability to adapt and innovate in order to create something new out of the interaction between people representing diverse points of view, worldviews, and frames of reference. It is the use of these pivotal capabilities that inspires a major fast food enterprise to sell muttonburgers in New Delhi and seaweed in Tokyo without lobbying hard to change the basic operation and infrastructure of the business.

Now you should understand better where we got the concept of the pivot. To add dimension to this understanding, imagine a globe of the world. You are standing in front of this globe. You locate your own country. You are an effective manager in your own country because you have the knowledge, abilities, skills, and experience that you need—the essential managerial capabilities. Now imagine that the globe starts spinning. That spinning globe represents what we mean by global complexity. Time, country borders, and culture are in motion. To be effective you must be able to adapt what you know to this spinning globe. You must take what you know and do it differently again and again and again. Think for a moment about the axis on which the globe spins. Just as the axis allows the globe to spin, the pivotal capabilities allow you to adapt what you know to the situation at hand. The spinning globe represents global complexity. The pivotal capabilities represent your axis—the capability to master this complexity.

1

The World of the Global Manager

John Smith is sitting at his desk in New York City. The phone rings. It is the British plant manager in Beijing announcing that the plant is closed down because the workers are demonstrating against the accidental bombing of their embassy in Belgrade. John accepts this information without comment. He does not know how alarmed he should be as he only knows this plant manager slightly and is not sure whether he is given to understatement or exaggeration. He has always found it hard to read the British.

John turns to his e-mail. There is a message from the plant manager in Mexico. Inflation remains rampant and employees are once again complaining that they are not making enough to pay their ever-increasing rent. John is mildly annoyed and responds abruptly, wondering at the same time whether he really should have hit the send button. These Mexican managers act like parents instead of managers.

The phone rings again. The Saudi Arab plant manager in the United Kingdom informs him, as an aside to the conversation, that consumers are becoming increasingly resistant to the idea of genetically engineered foods. John considers the possibility of halo—the spreading of antiglobalization sentiment. John leaves to go to a meeting and passes the director of finance in the hallway, who tells him that the relocation costs for expatriates are out of control. John hardly hears him. He still has Beijing on his mind.

John stops and turns back to his office to ask his secretary to arrange a conference call of all plant managers. This call will take place across twelve time zones. John knows this means that he will be up at 3 A.M. to participate in the call. The secretary reminds him that he will be flying to Mexico on Monday for a five-day stay and then going on to England for an additional week. She wants to know whether John wants the call scheduled before he goes or while he is traveling. (John has acquired in excess of a hundred thousand frequent flyer miles for the third year in a row but wonders if he will ever get to use them or if he even wants to.)

John once again heads out of the office back toward the meeting where he is on the agenda to explain the cost overruns in manufacturing.

John Smith is a new global manager. Like Peter in Shreveport, he is not an expatriate. John lives in New York, and his office is in New York, but he manages across distance, country borders, and cultural regions through the use of telephone, e-mail, fax, and frequent airplane trips. Every time John picks up a phone, gets off an airplane, or logs on to his e-mail, he is faced with a management issue—as is any manager—but John must assess and respond to each issue through the ever-shifting lens of distance, country, and culture.

Pick up any newspaper, read the latest article in the business press, or skim the recent business publications in your local bookstore and your eyes are certain to fall on the word *global*. Indeed, we are living in a unique place in history. Not since the Industrial Revolution has humanity encountered such powerful economic forces as those presently brought by the marriage of information technology and globalization. Succeeding in the global economy has risen to the top of many corporate agendas, and in increasing numbers, global managers such as John Smith are asked to lead the way.

Yet even for the John Smiths of the world, it is difficult to fully grasp the magnitude of change we are presently experiencing.

There has been trade between nations throughout history, but the *global economy*—in terms of a one-world market—is a phenomenon of the past several decades. In human terms, the global economy has come of age within the life span of a single generation of managers.

In the introduction to Part I, we talked about the notion of a globe spinning on its axis. In this first chapter, we want to stop this globe from spinning—if only for a brief moment—and take a detailed look at the world of the global manager. Before turning our attention to the capabilities required to be an effective global manager (in Chapters Two and Three) and before considering how to develop these capabilities (in Chapters Four and Five), we'd like to establish an understanding of the nature of global managerial work as it is increasingly practiced today. This understanding will set the stage for establishing what it takes to be effective and determining how to get there.

Throughout this chapter, we will discuss the world of the global manager through the eyes of John Smith. John is a fictional character, but in many ways his story is a common one for today's managers. His career has evolved with the transformations of the global economy. First, we will describe the world John began working in and how that world has changed. Second, we will describe current career demands with regard to distance, country, and culture. And third, we will discuss what it means to talk about managing effectively in this global world. We haven't forgotten Peter, though, and we will return to him later in the book. His is a different tale.

How Times Have Changed

After graduating from college with a business degree in 1972, John Smith began his career with EarthFoods as a junior sales representative at the Cleveland office. EarthFoods was one of the largest U.S. producers of packaged foods and had its products on grocery shelves from coast to coast. At this time there was some competition in the packaged foods industry, and EarthFoods was known for its highly recognizable products and keen understanding of the domestic market.

John's supervisor took an interest in his career development from the beginning. Since John was assigned a desk down the hall from his boss, it was easy for the two to get together to discuss U.S. market trends, resources, and environmental conditions. John learned a great deal about the business in a short time, and within a year he had taken his first business trip to the East Coast.

At the time, most businesses in the United States operated primarily from a domestic perspective, as they'd done since the end of World War II. U.S. businesses produced unique goods and services that were also marketed and sold almost exclusively in the United States. The unique qualities of the good or service and a lack of foreign competition resulted in a low priority for sensitivity to cultural differences within the U.S. market. Besides, this market was so large in comparison with other markets that it made sense to worry only about selling in the United States. At the start of his career, John saw culture as something that influenced his choice of color in shirt and tie, or something that was joked about with regard to California and New York City, rather than as something that reflected the language that people spoke, how they expected to be treated, or the religion they practiced.

Settling In

The 1980s were a time of great success for both John and Earth-Foods. The food industry was in a period of consolidation, and EarthFoods grew exponentially through a series of buy-outs, acquisitions, and strategic alliances. The 1980s also served as the first point in the company's history in which it marketed, produced, and sold its products abroad. During this time, John took on added responsibilities and was granted several promotions. He moved from sales into an assistant managerial position in production, and was later promoted to manage a large production facility on the outskirts of Los Angeles.

On the West Coast, John encountered his first taste of the larger world. He supervised employees from a variety of cultural backgrounds and interacted frequently with people whose first language was not English. He attended training sessions on cutting-edge Japanese quality management techniques. He participated in a focus group that examined international eating preferences and environmental conditions on Olvera Street in Los Angeles. He took international business trips and began to feel the pressures that were being exerted on the United States by international businesses.

During the late 1970s and 1980s, EarthFoods as well as other U.S. organizations began to take on an international perspective. Increased competition (both domestic and international) ushered in the need to export or assemble and produce goods abroad. Also, the markets abroad had expanded, and the increasing ease of transportation was making it worthwhile to take advantage of both lower costs abroad and the expanding markets. Many organizations continued to operate from a predominantly domestic orientation but now had an additional international component. Other organizations, particularly in competitive industries such as banking and technology, began to adopt a multinational approach in which domestic and global operations were integrated into worldwide lines of business. Although this approach represented a significant move toward a global focus, products and services were still largely standardized for the U.S. market (which was very large in comparison with the other markets), and strategy remained largely centralized in the home-country headquarters.

As globalization of the economy and John's managerial responsibility increased in the 1980s, he began to experience changes in the global complexity of his work; that is, he began managing across geographic distance, country infrastructures, and cultural expectations. John began to realize the need to develop a better understanding and appreciation of the norms, values, and work preferences of his employees. He realized that his peers and direct reports were increasingly likely to come from different countries and cultures and that he needed to have some idea of their perspectives.

He experienced the challenge of having telephone conversations with suppliers on the other side of the world. He realized that the American way was not the only way and, in some places, was not the best way of doing business. The world in which John began working was different from the one he'd worked in up until now. John's understanding of the world was changing too.

At the Top

The 1980s made recognition of the international arena common-place; the 1990s made it imperative. EarthFoods remained at the forefront of these trends within the food industry. By the mid-1990s, EarthFoods was rapidly being positioned as a competitive, global organization. Domestic and foreign operations were increasingly integrated, products were increasingly mass customized to country and cultural needs, and strategy was, to a much greater degree, distributed across the many countries in which EarthFoods conducted business.

To succeed within this environment, EarthFoods needed managers who were effective working across boundaries of distance, countries, and cultures. John Smith was ready for the challenge. At the end of the 1990s, John was appointed vice president for global production, with direct line responsibility that crisscrossed the planet.

Ian Mitroff (1987) has summed up today's competitive business environment in the following way: "For all practical purposes, all business today is global. Those individual businesses, firms, industries, and whole societies that clearly understand the new rules of doing business in a world economy will prosper; those that do not will perish." Also commenting on these trends, economist Robert Reich (1991) states that in the twenty-first century, "There will be no national products or technologies, no national corporations, no national industries. There will no longer be national economies, at least as we have come to understand that concept . . . all that will remain rooted within national borders are the people who comprise a nation."

Although these statements are certainly open to debate, it is clear that the traditional orientation of large businesses working solely within national boundaries is declining worldwide. More organizations daily are or are becoming global in their focus. The key characteristic, as defined by Christopher Bartlett and Sumantra Ghoshal (1989) in their seminal book *Managing Across Borders*, is that global organizations operate across national boundaries, simultaneously achieving global integration while retaining local differentiation.

Stephen Rhinesmith (1993) emphasizes that this characteristic of "thinking globally and acting locally" represents a wholly new paradigm for management. It requires organizational alignment along three broad dimensions: strategy and structure, corporate culture, and people. Of the three dimensions, people are the critical factor because it is through people that the strategy, structure, and corporate culture are enacted. Strategy, structure, and corporate culture cannot operate without people who can actually do the job of working efficiently and effectively across boundaries. In this era of global competition, managers like John Smith are ultimately the key to organizational success.

John's work—once confined within national boundaries—now takes place in many countries. Although the pace of his work leaves little time for reflection about how things have changed, his world has changed dramatically in the past thirty years. As a global manager, John now manages simultaneously across the boundaries of distance, countries, and cultures. This is a much more complex job than the one that faced someone in his position thirty years ago. For an idea of how the world is divided along the lines of distance, country, and culture, see Figure 1.1.

Distance. In managing across distance, John must deal with both the inconvenience of time differences and the significant psychological difficulty of working with people who cannot see one another. When he began his career with EarthFoods, the majority of his work activity was spent within the parameters of a single floor

FIGURE 1.1. Examples of Countries by Cultural Region.

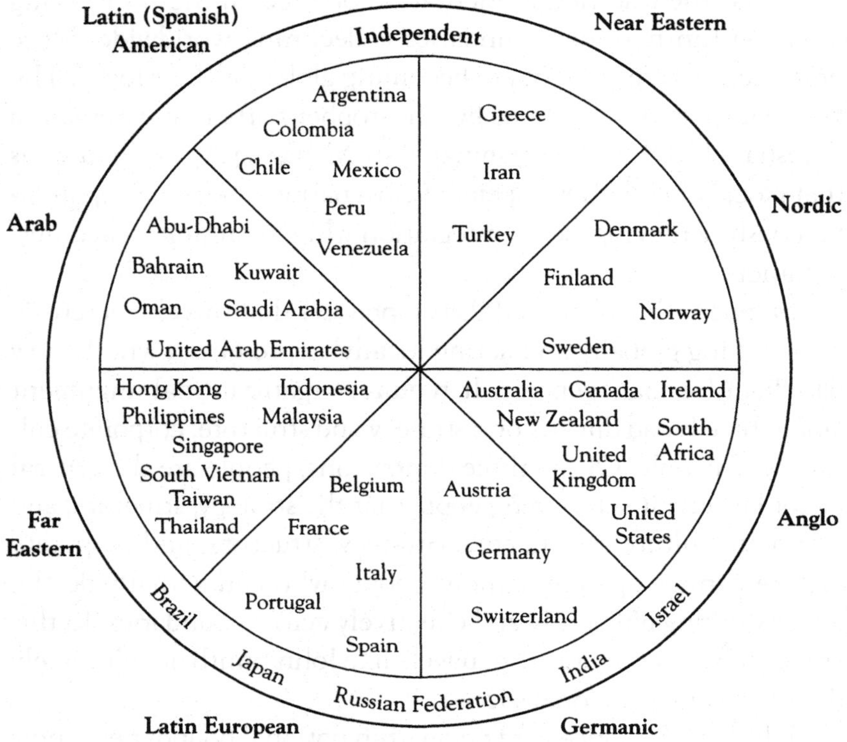

Source: Adapted from Ronen and Shenkar (1985), p. 449.

of an office building. His boss and peers were on the same hall. Meetings were held in the conference room. The telephone served as John's primary connection to the outside world.

Today, John has managerial responsibility in twelve time zones. He works largely in a virtual environment in which face-to-face contact is often impossible. Typical norms include handling fifty to seventy-five e-mail messages daily, meeting in person with subordinates once every six weeks, and working in airplanes and airports. In essence, John is a telecommuter across continents.

Furthermore, in working virtually, John often lacks visual cues to indicate how people respond to whatever information is being communicated. For example, John's brief and to-the-point e-mail note to the Mexican manager may have been interpreted as being anywhere from efficient to curt to dismissive. On his upcoming conference call, which requires John to be up at 3 A.M., the telephone will not allow him to observe visual cues such as heavy eyelids, doodles on scratch paper, or a cynical smirk at the other end of the line.

Country. In managing across countries, John must negotiate multiple variations in business infrastructures, political and economic systems, regulatory and legal frameworks, and civic and labor practices.

When John became the plant manager in Los Angeles, everyone shared a common understanding of basic business infrastructure. Although his employees were from different cultural backgrounds and countries, they all lived and worked in one country, the United States. Though their preferences about how things should work differed, they all knew that they were working within a U.S. system. They shared common daily experiences. In balancing a checkbook, they experienced the American financial system; in exercising the right to vote, they experienced the democratic political process; in selling their car to the highest bidder, they experienced capitalism; and in getting a speeding ticket in their new car, they learned about the law.

Now, as a global manager, John will not have the luxury of working with people who live in the same social system that he does. He must work with people outside the United States who live in different systems and who may have very different ideas about how business gets done. He must understand how differences among countries regarding unions, currency exchange rates, corporate governance, political legislation, investment policy, and technology transfer affect business processes. And in addition to understanding (or at least keeping in mind) these differences in systems, he must at the same time stay aware of and somehow deal with events occurring around the world over which he has no control. Inflation in Mexico, antiglobalization sentiment in the United Kingdom, and the accidental bombing of a Chinese embassy are events that are completely removed from John's sphere of influence, yet they can have a significant impact on his work.

Culture. In managing across cultures, John must take into account the complex interactions of norms, beliefs, values, and attitudes that distinguish one cultural group from another. Given the cultural diversity of the world, this is an extremely challenging task.

When John went to work out of college, cultural differences in the Cleveland office were not much of an issue. This changed for him when he became plant manager in Los Angeles. For the first time in his career, John had to interact with people who were culturally different and who frequently spoke a different language. He hadn't worked before in an environment where he couldn't understand people when he went to the shop floor. But that was the reality in Los Angeles, where employees often spoke to one another in their native language: Spanish, Thai, Kurdish, Vietnamese, Lebanese, Malay, Portuguese, French, Korean, and so forth. From working with these people he learned that there was no "one best way" to work with all people in all situations. Yet the extent of these differences was limited by the fact that all his employees were citizens of a single country and there was a single, dominant system.

Now, working globally, John must address multiple and differing expectations about how people (employees, colleagues, customers, suppliers, distributors) should behave, and how work should get done. From his uncertainty about how alarmed to be when the British plant manager calls about the plant closing in Beijing and his annoyance at a Mexican manager for getting so involved personally with his people, John understands that business works differently in different places. But because of the cultural differences he isn't sure what (if any) common ground exists.

Managing in a Context of Global Complexity

The term *global manager* defines managers by the context in which they work. Throughout the book, we describe this context as one of *global complexity*. To think more about what this means, consider the challenges that John faces working across geographic distance, country infrastructures, and cultural expectations. When we multiply each of these dimensions by the number of countries John manages and the variations among these countries, the complexity becomes even more evident. Indeed, it is the simultaneity of distance, countries, and cultures that most clearly distinguishes John's work today from his work at the start of his career.

For John's upcoming teleconference, there is a person from a different cultural background at the other end of each of those lines. When he hears about the plant closing in Beijing, he must hold this information in conjunction with the news he is receiving about inflation in Mexico, and the increasing resistance to genetically engineered foods in the United Kingdom. He doesn't just have one fire in one place to put out. He has fires in many different places that need different types of attention. Not only does John have to remember where the fires are, he also has to figure out what to do about them that won't cause the situations to get worse. And if he chooses a solution that is not culturally appropriate for the place where each fire is, he may end up with a worse problem than he started with.

Given this type of global complexity, all John can do on any given day is to ask himself: Where am I? Who is sitting across the table from me? And what do I need to do to be effective in this context?

What We Mean by Effectiveness

This book is about how to become an effective global manager. What do we mean by *effectiveness*? This seems like a straightforward question, because everybody knows what effectiveness is, don't they? But if you are a global organization, this is not a straightforward question, because different countries have very different ideas about what effectiveness is. For example, consider the following description, adapted from Derr and Laurent (1989, p. 296): *German managers believe that technical creativity and competence is essential for career success. The French and British view such managers as "mere technicians." The Dutch do not place high value on interpersonal relations and communications. The British see the ability to create the right image and get noticed for what they do as essential for career success. Americans value entrepreneurs. The British and French view entrepreneurial behavior as highly disruptive. The French view the ability to manage power relationships effectively and to "work the system" as critical to their career success.*

So what is effectiveness? It depends on where you are and who is around you. Understanding that culture influences what success and effectiveness look like, in this book and in the research study that supports this book we have attempted to define effectiveness in as multifaceted and culturally encompassing a way as possible. In other words, we have tried to come up with phrases that bosses and direct reports can use to rate the performance of the managers in our study that would not be too distorted by the lens of culture but would recognize that different cultures interpret effectiveness differently.

In this book effectiveness includes four factors: management and leadership, interpersonal relationships, knowledge and initiative, and success orientation. The exact questions that were used in our research are listed in Exhibit 1.1. We believe that this set of performance indicators captures to some extent the various lenses of effectiveness: ambition and entrepreneurialism, technical creativity, collaborative relationships, interpersonal skill, and the ability to manage power relationships.

We hope that the reader is gaining some appreciation for the notion that proficiency in some of the performance indicators will be more highly valued in one culture than another. Effectiveness is

EXHIBIT 1.1. What Do We Mean by Effectiveness?

Management and Leadership

Is able to establish and communicate common long-term goals.

Is an expert communicator.

Is an inspirational leader.

Is an excellent manager.

Excels at selecting and developing good people.

Consistently helps staff produce high-quality work.

Establishes and maintains good relationships with direct reports.

Manages conflict to enhance the quality of decisions.

Interpersonal Relationships

Works well with senior managers.

Has excellent relationships within the company.

Works well with peers and other departments to get the work done.

Works extremely well as a team member.

Knowledge and Initiative

Takes calculated entrepreneurial risks.

Demonstrates independence and initiative.

Has broad business knowledge of political, economic,
  and technological issues.

Demonstrates confidence in the face of ambiguity.

Is professionally competent.

Has superior knowledge of the business.

Success Orientation

Consistently drives for better outcomes.

Meets company goals and expectations for the position.

Could handle the most senior position in the company well.

Uses the complexity of the job to help produce innovative outcomes.

in the eye of the beholder. It doesn't matter how effective managers are perceived to be in their own country if their talents do not fit the cultural template of the observer. This is the reality of the global manager who lives in one place, whose boss is located in another, and whose direct reports are scattered all over the world. Effective global managers produce results that others in and outside the organization value, and they do it in ways that others in and outside the organization deem appropriate.

2

What You Already Know

Your Essential Capabilities

Peter is ready for the first meeting with his new team. They will meet via videoconference. Some members of the group are in France. The others are with him in the Shreveport office. Peter has decided not to connect all the people in the other U.S. offices, but the key people are in the room. Peter is particularly pleased that he has been able to establish the videoconference because the team members will be able to see each other. He knows that not all sites have videoconference facilities. It is a coup to have arranged it. He has read somewhere that the French value technology, and he hopes this videoconference will create a good first impression.

Peter is somewhat frustrated that the French team made what he considered to be a big fuss about the date of this meeting. He scheduled the meeting for the second week in August, and the French group complained bitterly about this encroachment on their vacation. Peter has had to change many family vacations because of work situations, and he is impatient with the people who complained about the timing of this meeting. It is, after all, the first meeting since the acquisition. He's surprised that they don't think it is as important as he does.

The technician makes the connection. Peter and his colleagues look up at the screen. They see a group of people sitting around a conference table with what appear to be neat stacks of paper in front of them. The room around the table is filled with easels holding graphs and charts. Everyone looks very serious. Peter greets and welcomes them and asks each of the group members sitting around the table in Shreveport to introduce himself or herself. These people oblige, introducing themselves by their first names and bantering and making jokes about their titles and responsibilities. When it is their turn, the managers in France introduce themselves, providing full names and titles, and each gives a relatively long and detailed account of individual responsibilities, accompanied by diagrams, graphs, and charts.

Peter notes with embarrassment and consternation that the U.S. contingent is not paying attention. They all seem to be making fun of the British accents of these English-speaking Frenchmen. Peter is relieved that most of this silent mocking seems to be out of camera range. He spends some time discussing the practical benefits of the acquisition for both entities and describes what he sees as the major issues facing them over the next few months. He ends the call by scheduling the next meeting, and he makes what he believes to be a very thoughtful comment wishing the French group a nice vacation. (He cannot resist letting them know that no one in the United States gets such a long vacation, because in his opinion the French group should really appreciate a long vacation as a perk rather than a right.)

When Peter gets off the phone and thinks about the meeting, he is concerned about the stiffness and formality of the French group. On his end of the line, the members of the U.S. contingent collapse in laughter and guffaws as soon as the line has been disconnected. "Did you ever hear such accents!" "Was that English they were speaking?" "What stuffed shirts!" "Do they really expect us to know all those details about our operation? We could never get our work done if we started micromanaging like that." "How urgent can this work be if these guys are all getting ready to go on vacation?" the U.S. managers say while leaving the meeting.

Peter has just had his first experience as a global manager. He chose to introduce the French and U.S. work groups to one another via technology rather than face to face because he felt that the organization would not consider the latter a good use of scarce resources. He failed to take into account that the members of each group might have some concerns about their own job security, and he was oblivious to the emotional undertones and ramifications of this meeting.

His U.S. colleagues think the meeting was "classic Peter." He has done what he does best: he has demonstrated that he is efficient, tactical, practical, and able to put the business first. Unfortunately, his new team in France has interpreted this same behavior as unseemly, hasty, ill-prepared, and rude. As a result, before they have even met in the same room both Peter and his newest direct reports are making negative attributions about one another's behavior based on a misunderstanding of intent compounded by distance.

But Peter is just doing what a manager does. He's trying to get the job done efficiently and cost-effectively. He had to do this when he was in a domestic position, and now he has to do it in his new global position. Managers have to do many of the same things whether their job is domestic or global—the difference is in how they do them.

In this chapter we will discuss the capabilities that are associated with high performance, whether the manager's responsibilities are global or domestic. Managers who got high performance ratings in our studies need these capabilities. We recount them here so that you can assess your own ability to use these skills in your own work.

Some of the activities that you have been doing for years in a domestic setting are also critical in your role as a global manager. You don't have to start from scratch—you probably already have the important skills that you need to carry out these activities. We call them the five *essential managerial capabilities*. We will describe them and give you the tools to identify these assets in yourself. But first, a word about why they are important.

Same But Different

We characterize the five essential managerial capabilities as "same but different" because these capabilities are things that managers need whether they are working only in their own country or working simultaneously across distance, countries, and cultures. They are

- The ability to manage people
- The ability to manage action
- The ability to manage information
- The ability to cope with pressure
- Core business knowledge

A manager plays the same roles but the behaviors and the knowledge associated with the roles are different when working in a global setting. For example, if you disagreed with your boss, would you state your disagreement in the same manner in Tokyo with Japanese coworkers as you would in The Hague with Dutch coworkers? We hope not. Though you would be getting the same point across, how you would get it across would have to change drastically because of what kind of behavior is considered acceptable in each of those places.

The need to do the same thing in a different way can create real tension for the practicing manager. Managers are often promoted to complex global jobs because they are very good at what they do. They often have a history of technical and professional expertise, timely promotions, strong records of success domestically, and a long string of accomplishments. They are accustomed to success.

However, if not modified to meet the situation, the behaviors that worked in one place and led to the promotion to a global job will become the weaknesses that lead to failure in the global job. If managers do not adapt to the global nature and increased complexity of their jobs, they may fail because they are continuing to do what has worked before without adapting to circumstances and culture. They are not thinking about how to do what needs to be done in a way that will succeed in the new context. Global managers must learn to adapt their strengths and use them differently, and they need to help others learn to do the same.

As we have already stated, effective managers, whether their work is domestic or global, must be skilled at managing people, action, and information. These roles were first outlined by Henry Mintzberg in his classic book, *The Nature of Managerial Work*, published in 1973. What Mintzberg said is that what managers do will be the same regardless of their function, their industry, or the economic conditions. Managers have to do what managers have to do.

However, Mintzberg also said that one set of roles may be more critical than another, depending on the context. Effective managers must be able to shift focus from one role to another in response to the needs at the moment. They must be able to know when to concentrate on people, when to concentrate on action, when to concentrate on communication, and so forth. For example, in good economic times managers may need to concentrate on people; during such times employees have lots of choices and managers need to work hard to hang onto their best talent. Consider the phrase "war for talent," which gained currency from 1995 to 2000 as a way to describe how difficult it was for a company to recruit and retain talented people. Companies spent a lot of time and effort to become the employer of choice. In harsh economic times managers are in an emergency mode. They are trying to survive. They are focused on cutting costs and finding new efficiencies and economies of scale. Even the most people-focused organizations have layoffs and freeze hiring. They may do it more humanely than other companies, but their focus is on action.

We take this idea one step further. Effective global managers must not only know when one set of roles is relatively more critical than another and be able to concentrate in the right areas, they must also be able to adapt how they play their roles as a function of the context they are in and be able to read the cues they get from others correctly. No matter how skillfully managers have learned to play each of the managerial roles in their own countries, managing within a global context creates new needs, requirements, expectations, and demands. Managers must be able to recognize these and respond accordingly.

In addition to thinking about where they are and to whom they are talking, managers with global responsibilities must demonstrate and use each of these capabilities differently as a function of the varying structural characteristics of the situation. For example, much of the time they may be working through technology, and that decontextualized form of communication will need to be treated differently from a face-to-face meeting. They may also be working within and across a variety of legal and political systems, which they probably don't know as well as their own. This change in the basic structure of general systems may require significant changes in behavior. For example, managers' conduct with bankers, government officials, and labor union representatives will be different in almost every country they work in.

Finally, managers with global responsibilities are working with people who expect them to behave differently from the way they naturally would at home and may misunderstand what they do. And the reverse is also true. The people in unfamiliar locations will not behave as the managers expect, and the managers are also likely to misunderstand why the people do what they do.

Returning to Peter, it is clear that he is going to have to be willing and able to adapt his behavior so that his new French colleagues are more comfortable with him, as will his new French colleagues, in turn. Finally, Peter is going to have to learn to act as an intermediary by helping the people at home adapt to the French, and vice versa. Communicating across distance was probably not the best way to have begun. Though a videoconference is better than e-mail or the phone, it does not provide enough nonverbal cues to make communication in these circumstances anything but difficult. The awkwardness and poor first impression created by style differences (formal versus informal) are exacerbated by the conflicting cultural emphasis on detail versus knowledge of the big picture. These factors, coupled with the difficult circumstances (merger and potential concerns about the future) and different cultural expectations, made it almost impossible for the meeting to succeed.

Peter and the members of his work group left their first encounter with a sense of foreboding based on the meaning they attributed to one another's behavior. All the participants in that videoconference interpreted what happened through their own lens and the lens of their culture.

On one hand, the French coworkers thought Peter rude because his behavior indicated that he did not appreciate the importance of the French tradition of the August family vacation. On the other hand, Peter thought the French coworkers did not demonstrate sufficient commitment to their work because they complained about a brief disruption of their vacation. The French considered Peter and the rest of the American team shockingly superficial and uninformed because they didn't describe the details of their work. Peter and the American team thought that the French were absurdly and unnecessarily focused on minutiae. Team members on either side of the ocean made no connection with one another at all, except to evaluate the others as inappropriate, uninformed, rude, and strange. How were they ever going to be able to work with people like that?

For Peter to be successful as a manager with global responsibilities he will need to do what he has always done—manage, lead, communicate, act—but he will need to do each of these things differently to bridge the cultural differences.

In the following sections we will describe and define in greater depth the five essential managerial capabilities, mentioned earlier in the chapter, that we found to be critical to performance whether a manager's work is global or domestic: ability to manage people, action, and information; ability to cope with pressure; and core business knowledge. We will give examples of what we mean when we say that those who are managing people, action, and information across distance, country borders, and cultural expectations must be prepared to account for this global complexity in very specific ways.

We then introduce a set of tools you can use to analyze a globally complex situation, anticipate what to expect, and plan how to adapt your own behavior. We will discuss the tools for each dimension of global complexity that we discussed in Chapter One: distance, country infrastructure, and cultural expectations. Keep in mind that the global manager must employ all these tools at once.

Five Essential Capabilities of Effective Managers

We assume that you, the reader, are already a reasonably effective manager in your own country. We expect that you already have the five essential managerial capabilities: you know how to manage people, action, and information; you can cope with pressure; and you possess core business knowledge. As we discuss each capability, think about how you demonstrate that skill now and how you would alter your behavior to get the same result in situations in which your typical behavior would not work effectively.

Ability to Manage People

When we talk about managing people in organizations, we are talking about the ability to motivate people to do the best job they can. We are talking about the ability to collaborate and influence others inside and outside the organization who are not direct reports or bosses. And we are talking about an organization's practices that reflect the ability of a manager to motivate and influence—the practices associated with recruitment, selection, development, appraisal, and promotion.

To be an effective manager of people a manager must influence others and move them toward the accomplishment of organizational goals, whether employees are ten feet or ten thousand miles away. Most managers know how to do this if people are ten feet or even a hundred miles away, but the task is much more complex if the distance is great and the country and culture are different.

One of the reasons effective management becomes more difficult is the way distance increases differences in how people understand and make sense of the world around them. Peter Smith, Mark Peterson, and Shalom Schwartz (forthcoming) describe the need for managers to "make sense" of what is going on in ways that "make sense" to those they are attempting to influence. Managers who are attempting to influence their work group or their peers and colleagues in ways that don't make sense to the peers and colleagues will fail. Culture is one way people make sense of the world, and misunderstanding culture is one reason a manager may fail to make sense to others.

Ability to Manage Action

Managing action includes two major types of activities: decision making and negotiation and conflict management. Skill in the role of decision maker involves taking action, knowing how much information is required to take action, knowing who to involve in the decision process, being willing to modify decisions, being willing to make decisions that call for organizational change, and making timely decisions. Skill as a negotiator and conflict manager includes being able to help groups with views or needs in conflict set priorities, share resources, and find common ground and a productive resolution.

Skill in the role of decision maker was the most powerful predictor of high performance ratings of any of the variables in the Center for Creative Leadership's global research study, regardless of whether the job was local or global. Unfortunately, as we will illustrate in the Tools section, beginning on page 37, decision making is strongly affected by culture and distance.

Ability to Manage Information

Monitoring information, keeping track of information, serving as an external spokesperson for the organization, and communicating information throughout the organization are all part of the ability to manage information. But managing information doesn't work the same way everywhere. Different countries and cultures have different rules about who can have what information and when, and how that information needs to be communicated. What is likely to be different as a result of cultural variation includes who gets to have the information, the order in which the information is disseminated, who gets to provide the information to whom, the willingness to communicate the information, the nuance of language, the meaning or emotional impact of the information, and the ability to disagree with the message.

Ability to Cope with Pressure

All managers should be adept at coping with pressure, because their jobs typically demand long hours, the integration of huge amounts of information, work performed on the run, and hours spent in airports and airplanes away from home and familiar surroundings. The first adaptation that may be required of effective managers with domestic or global responsibilities is to examine how they deal with pressure and, if necessary, change how they deal with it. If, for example, managers eat too much, smoke too much, drink too much, sleep too little, and exercise infrequently, there is ample evidence to suggest that not only are they risking their health, they are also probably making themselves less effective as managers.

A study conducted by Sharon McDowell and Judith Steed at the Center for Creative Leadership with CEOs and their direct reports found that managers with better health were also better managers (2000). Traits such as low cholesterol levels and low blood pressure were correlated with higher performance ratings. And so as a manager, you should examine your response to pressure. You may need to adopt stress-reduction strategies that are less harmful than overeating, smoking, or drinking. This becomes even more critical when your work is globally complex.

Core Business Knowledge

A strong fundamental understanding of how the business works is critical for all managers, whether their work is global or local. In our CCL study, managers who were described as effective knew the business, and that held true for both local and global managers.

Though it is equally important to have business knowledge whether the work is domestic or global, the meaning of business knowledge is different for domestic and global managers. To manage globally, managers must try to understand what customers, vendors, and suppliers who are culturally different want, what the country systems and structures will allow, and what the distance requires. (See Chapter Three for more on gaining international business knowledge.)

The Tools

The essential managerial capabilities are critical to both local and global managers. But being good at something when you are a domestic manager does not mean that you will be good at it as a global manager. As we have already said, the roles you have to play and the things you have to accomplish are fundamentally the same, but the knowledge and behaviors associated with getting the work done are not necessarily the same in the different contexts.

We have put together a set of tools to help you understand how to modify your behavior in response to the demands of global work. We characterize these tools according to the three dimensions of global managerial work discussed in Chapter One: geographic distance, country infrastructure, and cultural expectations.

Distance

Technology is the vehicle that has made much of the work of global managers possible. Without fax machines, improvements in telecommunication, the Internet, the Web, the PC, the Palm Pilot, and perhaps even other devices invented since this book went to press, we would not be writing this book because there would be no need for it. Globalization would not have moved beyond the establishment of far-flung franchises, semiautonomous offshore operations, and elaborate import-export and distribution schemes. An integrated global entity that allows managers to work simultaneously across multiple time zones, country borders, and cultures (and demands that they do so) would not and could not have existed thirty years ago in the same way it does now.

The confusion resulting from this exposure to different customs, laws, and practices would not have been a daily reality for a general manager thirty years ago. The potential for mistakes, missteps, and even disasters would have been lessened exponentially. In the past, businesspeople traveled across the ocean on ships or planes to have meetings. They made expensive long-distance calls with uncertain connections when they absolutely had to talk to somebody. They had time to think about what they were going to do and how they were going to do it before they took action. Integration of processes and practices was not leveraged as a business advantage—it was not even possible.

Technology has changed the nature of work because it has made it faster, it has increased the complexity of work because it has made it broader, and it has changed how managers must do their work because the whole nature of the business has changed. People no longer *have* to be in the same place to work together; frequently they have never met the people who pass them work. But they are not as free from the need for face-to-face or high-contact interaction as they would often prefer to believe.

It's tempting to believe that people can actually understand each other and communicate effectively through e-mail and the telephone. It would be useful if people did not need nonverbal cues to communicate. But the reality is that humans have evolved to need certain cues to understand others, and those cues are simply not available through the current technology. Though video and three-dimensional technologies are improving every day, they currently do not supply enough of the nonverbal cues that people need to really understand what is going on.

So what happens when people use technology and miss the cues? In Exhibit 2.1 we list some issues—intended and unintended—that tend to occur when technology is used to manage across distance. In Exhibit 2.2 we provide a tool that you may use when considering how you may need to manage differently (refer to our discussion of "same but different") across distance. Please keep in mind for the discussions that follow under "Country Infrastructure" and "Culture" that Exhibit 2.1 provides a cross-reference between the dimensions of distance and culture. Also note that the tips on Exhibit 2.2 can apply to managers working virtually, whether the work is global or domestic.

Country Infrastructure

Some people believe that the globalization of business will eventually result in a completely different legal, political, and economic infrastructure—that is, an entity larger than and different from the laws, politics, and economic systems of any one nation. They believe that the operations of global corporations will become more similar than different and that a global managerial culture will emerge. For some, this belief arises out of the perspective that the policies, procedures, and practices of their own country (and company) are the correct ones, so they work very hard to implement consistent policies and practices across country borders. For others, the belief comes from the perspective that through change, trial and error, and learning from others, a middle way will evolve because it is more efficient and practical.

Still others believe that the idea of a global managerial culture is a myth. They believe that the historical, legal, political, and economic frameworks underpinning the country of origin will maintain the greatest influence over the operations of an organization, regardless of globalization. They say that even if two organizations have a global strategy, the way each goes about implementing

EXHIBIT 2.1. Managing Across Distance: The Issues.

Issues likely to interact with culture

- It is easier to share knowledge than ever before.
- Decision making can become less hierarchical because knowledge is more easily shared.
- A twenty-four-hour work cycle is possible, providing a competitive edge in the information and service industries.
- Time lags are reduced.
- Geographically dispersed people behave differently:
  - They are less socially inhibited in their interactions (misattributions based on culture may lead to unfortunate and hasty electronic responses).
  - They are less hierarchical.
  - People are less likely to change their minds or give up their position (which makes negotiation and problem solving even more difficult).
  - Explicit coordination becomes more critical.
  - The development of trust may be inhibited (as with cultural difference).
  - Dispersed people communicate less frequently than do people who are co-located (when more communication is what they need).
- Communications are more task oriented.
- Some people participate more than others.
- Some people gain more influence than others.
- Dispersed groups have a harder time dealing with conflict and achieving consensus (confounded by cultural differences and misattributions).
- Dispersed people may have inaccurate perceptions of one another (confounded by cultural differences and misattributions).
- The links between people may be weaker (as with culture).
- There are no social cues in an interaction (tone of voice, facial expression, body language).

Issues likely to interact with country

- People who need to work together may have unequal access to technology or unequal expertise in the use of technology.
- There is less expense associated with travel, office space, and redundancy of resources (strong laws about termination and downsizing).

Issues with implications for development

- People can be recruited from anywhere in the world—wherever the talent is. (But will they be given the opportunity to advance?)
- There is better access to experts. (How to transfer knowledge?)
- There is the potential for greater job flexibility.

Other

- Greater collaboration and interdependence is possible.
- Dispersed groups take more time to accomplish goals if the work is interdependent.
- Members of dispersed interdependent teams are not as satisfied with their team membership.

Source: Adapted from Sessa, Hansen, Prestridge, and Kossler (1999), with permission.

EXHIBIT 2.2. Tips for Managing Across the Issues of Distance.

Managing Action

Establish norms for how you will make decisions.

Establish norms for how you will handle urgent decisions; for instance, how long you will wait to hear from everyone.

Managing People

Meet in person early in the process.

Recognize the inconvenience of doing business in different time zones.

Pay more attention to interpersonal issues.

Give difficult feedback in person.

Take into account that individuals have different levels of comfort and familiarity with technology.

Managing Information

Find out how each person prefers to communicate (phone, fax, e-mail, and so forth).

Establish norms for how urgent information will be communicated.

Set agendas in advance.

If someone joins a session late, don't recap for the whole team.

Plan for everything to take more time than it would if you were working face-to-face.

---

the strategy will reflect the laws and business practices of its country of origin.

Regardless of who turns out to be right, the implications for global managers are the same. They must be able to adapt and change what they do best in response to the context of the situation.

An interesting example of both points of view is provided in a December 13, 2000, article in the *Wall Street Journal* about Volkswagen Company. On one hand, this company is being pressed to adopt business practices that emphasize shareholder value. On the other hand, the company has thrived because it produces good cars at a reasonable cost, and it does this within the laws, culture, and values of Germany.

Klaus Seifert, a silver haired thirty-four-year VW veteran, enjoys a sterling record as an electronics planner. . . . He also has ironclad job protection. And he earns more than 100,000 marks for working four 7.5 hour days a week. "I know people say we are expensive and inflexible, but they are really missing the point. We make really good cars." What about making good profits? For years, the answer hardly mattered to VW. The automaker long worried much more about Mr. Seifert and its over 100,000 German workers than about its shareholders. So what if the company's profit margins were half those of smaller European rivals and if fund managers called it "communist"? VW's largest shareholder, the northern German state of Lower Saxony, has never complained; it has always been more concerned about jobs than share prices. Now Ferdinand Piech, who became VW's chairman in 1993, says the company is changing. His goal, he insists, is to earn profits as impressive as its products. . . . But can Europe's largest automaker really play by Wall Street rules? And should it? [Miller, 2000, pp. A21-A22].

How would a manager from the United States working with a boss in Germany reconcile the notion of worker protection with the goal of maximizing profits? How can Mr. Piech put the goals and objectives (profits) ahead of the laws of the country where VW is located? The tools for thinking about how to manage across country infrastructures—the legal, political, and historical information needed to make appropriate and legal decisions—may be the easiest to access. You can find information in books, CD-ROMs, universities, special courses, and from consultations with a company's legal, human resources, or finance department. What is interesting and frequently frightening is how often managers fail to make use of this information. They fly off to do business in someone else's country with little or no knowledge of the history, geography, or political systems of the place they are about to visit and where they will work.

We are not going to provide you here with a list of all possible laws and practices that might have an impact on the way to do business in a given country. Instead, we have a list of useful references in the back of the book (see, for example, the Suggested Reading section for Brake & Walker, 1995; and the References section for Bartlett & Ghoshal, 1989; Doremus et al., 1998) and we provide two tables to use as you manage across country borders.

Table 2.1 summarizes practices associated with industrial relations in the British, Latin European, and German-Nordic countries of Europe. Although the table is limited to the labor-relations practices of countries in three regions of Europe, it is illustrative of the connection among history, culture, and employee relations practices.

Table 2.2 illustrates how the (culturally determined) relationship between financial institutions, business, and the government

TABLE 2.1. Managing Across Country Borders: National Context and Employee Relations.

	British	Latin European	German-Nordic
Level of government intervention	Very limited	High and authoritarian	High and collaborative
Labor relations	Voluntarism: employees and trade unions develop their own rules and practices	Often combative	Harmonious and required by law
Bargaining position	Employees are individual contractors	There are often intense labor conflicts	Employees are integrated into the decision-making process of the firm

Source: Adapted from Hammer (1999). Used with permission of Elsevier Science.

in a given country determines business practices and laws. The table contrasts Germany, Japan, and the United States. Table 2.2 is not and cannot be all-inclusive, but it illustrates what we mean when we talk about the second dimension of global complexity: managing across country infrastructures. In using Tables 2.1 and 2.2 we invite you to consider these influences on the company you work in and the various countries in which you are managing or aspire to manage.

Culture

Social scientists have spent decades trying to understand how cultures differ. This has been a difficult task because *country* and *culture* do not necessarily mean the same thing. A country usually incorporates people of more than one cultural orientation. Even though one culture in a country is usually dominant or more prevalent than others, the dominant culture will coexist with a number of subcultures. This is just as true in the United States as it is in other countries. Just consider various regions of the country. The culture in the South is very different from that in the Northeast. The culture in Southern California is different from that in Northern California, and they are both different from that of New York City. The Midwest has its own culture, but there are distinctions that can be made between the cultures in Wisconsin and Indiana and Iowa. The United States and many other countries also have many cultures within a region based on gender, ethnic, or religious affiliations. Just because there is one country, one system, and one language doesn't mean that you don't have to negotiate your way through many different cultures. In addition, due to the influence of shared religion, shared history, and shared language, culture can be larger than a single country. In other words, countries encompass a number of cultures, and cultures encompass a number of countries.

Tagliabue (2001) outlines the dilemma that results by describing the clashes Toyota encountered between the group orientation of Japan and the individualistic orientation of France. For example,

TABLE 2.2. Managing Across Country Borders: National Context and Multinational Behavior.

Context	United States	Germany	Japan
Corporate governance	Short-term shareholding; managers highly constrained by capital markets; risk-seeking, financial-centered strategies	Managerial autonomy except during crises; little takeover risk; conservative long-term strategies	Stable shareholders; network-constrained managers; takeover risk only within network; aggressive market-share-centered strategies
Corporate finance	Diversified, global funding; highly price sensitive	Concentrated, regional funding; limited price sensitivity	Concentrated, national funding; low price sensitivity
Innovation system	Mission-oriented policy environment; mixed public and private funding and R&D performance; strong linkages across higher education and industry; high foreign R&D funding; national focus on science-intensive, high-tech industries	Diffusion-oriented policy environment; industry-centered funding and R&D performance with moderate public sector role; strong industry linkages; low foreign funding of R&D; national focus on specialized supplier and scale-intensive, medium-tech industries	Mixed policy environment (diffusion; mission); industry-centered funding and R&D performance, with low public sector role; strong interindustry linkages; very low foreign funding of R&D; national focus on specialized supplier and scale-intensive, medium-tech industries
Investment system	Liberal; no constraints on inward or outward direct investment	Modified liberal; indirect constraints on inward, no constraints on outward direct investment	Resistant; formal and informal constraints on inward, selective constraints on outward direct investment

Behavior	United States	Germany	Japan
Research and development	Centralized; larger overseas presence (especially in Germany and United Kingdom); growing slowly; high R&D intensity of foreign affiliates (especially in Germany)	Centralized; moderate overseas presence, growing steadily; high R&D intensity of foreign affiliates	Centralized; smaller, quickly growing overseas presence; low R&D intensity of foreign affiliates
Technology trade	Centralized; export oriented (large trade surplus)	Centralized; exchange oriented (balanced trade)	Centralized; acquisition oriented (large unaffiliated imports, low exports)
Technology alliances	Large number; mostly intra-U.S.	Moderate number, mostly Europe-U.S. and regional manufacturing, wholesale trade	Small number, mostly Japan-U.S.
Outward investment	Manufacturing, finance, services	Manufacturing, wholesale trade	Wholesale trade
Intrafirm trade	Moderate	Moderate to high	High
Local production	High integration	Moderate integration	Low integration

Source: Doremus, Keller, Pauly, and Reich (1998). Reprinted by permission of Princeton University Press.

the French value education and degrees but Toyota's strategy for its French plant is to recruit unskilled workers and train them. Toyota has a culture that emphasizes "we," but the French value "I" and so have no desire to wear the free company work clothes. The French value the trappings of privilege. Toyota does not provide private office space, much less a corporate dining room. Toyota is accustomed to a close and harmonious working relationship among the company, the government, the financial system, and the unions. According to French law they are required to install trade union representatives on their company labor board, and these relationships are often adversarial. And finally, the greatest clash of all—Toyota is forced to justify to the labor ministry its ban on red wine in the company cafeteria.

To understand the influence of culture within or across countries, social scientists have had to stand back from individuals and consider people as a group, a society, an average, a whole. These social scientists wanted to be able to understand whether there were ways of explaining the values and behaviors of groups of people that would be characteristic of one culture but not another. They wanted to be able to articulate the tacit norms, rules, and expectations that influence behavior and are shared by people in a culture. As a result of this work, many different frameworks have been developed to explain how cultures differ from one another.

Table 2.3 shows one of these cultural frameworks, the 7-D model of culture. The 7-D model was developed by Wilson, Hoppe, and Sayles (1996) and was recently updated by Hoppe (2000). It is based on a review of the work of the most prominent half-dozen cultural scholars and identifies the common elements and themes in all their work. (See other references in the References and Suggested Reading sections.)

Table 2.3 illustrates seven dimensions on which cultures differ:

- *Source and expressions of identity:* An individual's likely identification with self or a group.

- *Source and expressions of authority:* The opportunity to achieve a role of authority through hard work or through the rank accorded to one's birth.
- *Means and goals of achievement:* The meaning people give to work in relationship to the totality of life's experiences.
- *Response to uncertainty and change:* The societal value placed on certainty and stability versus a more entrepreneurial and opportunistic orientation.
- *Means of knowledge acquisition:* Preference for learning through observation versus learning through action and experimentation.
- *Orientation to time:* Time as a scarce commodity to be rationed versus time as a cyclical and seasonal phenomenon to be experienced.
- *Response to natural and social environment:* The cultural value placed on mastery versus the value placed on living in harmony within the natural and social environment.

Table 2.4 presents a number of countries ranked by where they fall on the seven dimensions. A cultural value is more descriptive for countries in the groupings that fall in the clusters at the top or bottom of the graph. A cultural value is not as descriptive for the countries near the middle of the graph. Together, Tables 2.3 and 2.4 can be used as tools for anticipating the impact of cultural expectations.

To become familiar with this tool, jot down the characteristics that you believe represent an effective manager in your country and then locate these characteristics within the descriptions on Table 2.3. For example, the prototypical American manager might be described as being individualistic and entrepreneurial, believing that everyone can make it to the top through hard work, sacrificing family life for work, and acting with an air of urgency and haste. Time is money! These adjectives would fall into the Individual, Tough, Equal, Dynamic, and Scarce dimensions. Though the value placed on these characteristics may vary as viewed

TABLE 2.3. Summary Descriptions of Seven Cultural Orientations.

Source and Expressions of Identity	Source and Expressions of Authority	Means and Goals of Achievement	Response to Uncertainty and Change	Means of Knowledge Acquisition	Orientation to Time	Response to Natural and Social Environment
Collective (emphasis on in-group)	*Equal* (equality by birth)	*Tender* (work to live)	*Dynamic* (comfort with uncertainty)	*Reflective* (learning by observation)	*Scarce* (time as linear)	*Being* (concern with harmony)
This dimension spells out the degree to which members of a country define themselves either by the group or organization to which they belong or by their own individual achievements. Members in countries near the "collective" end define themselves more in terms of the organization, tribe, clan, or extended family to which they belong. They expect, and are expected, to show loyalty and support toward their group or organization in return for protection, lifetime employment, and a sense of belonging.	This dimension describes a society's response to inequality in power among its members. In societies that highly value equality, people have come to expect differences in power among them to be minimized. Those with and without power alike see themselves as existentially equal and consider hierarchical structures as an expression of inequality in roles, established for convenience or efficiency. They want "superiors" to be accessible and to consult with them. They prefer a resourceful democrat with competence and a track record.	This dimension captures the different ways in which members of different societies define success and the ways of achieving it. Men and women in more "tender"-oriented societies place greater value on intangible achievements, such as good work relationships, time for family and friends, or doing something that helps others. They strive for cooperation, consensus, and solidarity among members of their own and others' society. They feel for the less fortunate and value being. They prefer the slogan 'work to live' over 'live to work.'	This dimension defines the degree to which the majority of a country prefers formal rules and explicitly structured activities to deal with unclear or unpredictable situations. In societies near the "dynamic" pole of the dimension, people accept uncertainty or ambiguity as a natural part of life. They do not shy away from conflict, dissent, or competition; in fact, they view them as potentially beneficial. They value flexibility, adaptability, and change and are open to adjusting existing rules or regulations as deemed necessary by the situation. They are willing to take risks even in unfamiliar circumstances.	This dimension depicts the preferred process or means by which members of different societies acquire information and knowledge. It is conceptually closely related to the "dynamic–stable" scale. Men and women from more "reflective"-oriented societies feel a greater need for conceptual models to guide their actions. They prefer to think things through, understand the general principles behind the problem, or develop an intuitive feel for it before attempting a solution. They admire intellectual brilliance and deductive reasoning. Overall, they favor great thinkers over doers.	This dimension helps illustrate the various ways in which different societies think of and deal with the passage of time. People from countries near the "scarce" side of the scale treat time as a limited resource that ought not to be wasted. They prefer to spend it purposefully and with intensity. They want meetings to start on time, and they want to stay busy and see results in the short term. They have a sense that every minute counts. They prefer to go about their tasks sequentially (monochronic), working in the present toward the future.	This dimension gauges the degree to which people from different societies try to gain mastery over the world around them. People from countries toward the "being" end of the dimension feel a need to live in unity with, as well as within the given limits of, their natural surroundings. They see themselves as a part of the world and accept what life gives them. They prefer a steady and relaxed way of life that allows them to live in the here and now. They trust that things will work out in the greater scheme of things. Harmony with, not mastery over, the world around them is seen as most important.

Source and Expressions of Identity	Source and Expressions of Authority	Means and Goals of Achievement	Response to Uncertainty and Change	Means of Knowledge Acquisition	Orientation to Time	Response to Natural and Social Environment
Individual (emphasis on self)	*Unequal* (inequality by birth)	*Tough* (live to work)	*Stable* (discomfort with uncertainty)	*Active* (learning by experimentation)	*Plentiful* (time as cyclical)	*Doing* (concern with mastery)
In societies near the "individual" end of the dimension, people look primarily after their own interest and that of their immediate family. They expect, and are expected, to be self-reliant, show self-initiative, and chart their own career.	Members of societies close to the "unequal" end of the dimension expect and accept large differences in power, status, and privileges. They view inequality among them as existential in nature. Hierarchies are considered an expression of this inequality, satisfying people's need for dependence, structure, and a sense of security. They prefer their superior to be a benevolent autocrat who takes the initiative, makes the decisions, and takes care of their needs.	In countries close to the "tough" end of the dimension, men and women alike strive for tangible success and progress, such as high income, career advancement, or working for a prestigious company. They value in themselves and others ambition, competitiveness, and decisiveness. They want to excel and have great admiration for the achiever. Work (or the "job") plays the central role in their lives.	Members of countries toward the "stable" end of the dimension are more likely to shun unfamiliar risks or unpredictable situations. They get nervous when encountering changes, conflict, or competition in their work and will try to avoid them in the first place through clearly defined rules, regulations, and policies. Theirs is an existential angst that makes them feel stressed and compelled to eschew mistakes and failure.	People from countries that favor an "active" approach value facts, empirical data, and practical experience. They are willing to experiment and solve problems by trial and error. Case studies, experiential learning, or fieldwork appeal to them. Overall, the scientific approach to identifying and solving problems feels natural to them.	Members of societies with a more "plentiful" orientation to time think of it as a "flowing river" or as infinitely available. Therefore, time cannot be wasted. Timeliness or deadlines are seen as an expression of intent, not as commitments. There is always a tomorrow. They prefer a life that evolves from the moment and allows for multiple and simultaneous involvement with the people and opportunities around them (polychronic). They honor the past to fully live in the present.	People in societies with a clear preference for "doing" want to actively shape their lives and surroundings. They value planful activities that improve their conditions. Technology is cherished as a means of making progress toward a better or more fulfilled life. Being in control over one's life and environment is seen as a quintessential value.

Source: Center for Creative Leadership. Adapted from version produced by Michael Hoppe, 2000. Not for reproduction or circulation without permission by CCL.

TABLE 2.4. Selected Countries and the Seven Cultural Dimensions.

Collective (emphasis on in-group)	Equal (equality by birth)	Tender (work to live)	Dynamic (comfort with uncertainty)	Reflective (learning by observation)	Scarce (time as linear)	Being (concern with harmony)
Indonesia	Sweden	Sweden	Singapore	Chile	United States	Italy
South Korea	United Kingdom	Chile	Sweden	France	United Kingdom	Turkey
Singapore	Germany	South Korea	United Kingdom	Spain	Canada	Spain
Chile	Canada	Egypt	India	Russia	Germany	France
Saudi Arabia	United States	Russia	United States	South Korea	Poland	Russia
Mexico			Canada	Turkey	South Africa	Sweden
Nigeria			Indonesia	Egypt	Sweden	Mexico
			South Africa	Saudi Arabia	Japan	
			Poland	Mexico	France	
				Brazil	Italy	
				Japan	Chile	
				Argentina	Argentina	
Egypt	Argentina	Spain	Nigeria	Iran	South Korea	Germany
Turkey	South Africa	Iran	Iran	Nigeria	Turkey	Poland
Brazil	Italy	France	Germany	Indonesia	Russia	Brazil
Iran	Poland	Turkey	Egypt	Italy	Singapore	Singapore
Japan	Japan	Indonesia		India	Brazil	
Argentina	Spain	Singapore		Singapore	Nigeria	
Russia	Iran	Brazil		Germany		

Individual (emphasis on self)	Unequal (inequality by birth)	Tough (live to work)	Stable (discomfort with uncertainty)	Active (learning by experimentation)	Plentiful (time as cyclical)	Doing (concern with mastery)
India	South Korea	Canada	South Africa			
Spain	Chile	Argentina				
	Turkey	India				
Poland	France	Nigeria	Italy	Sweden	Mexico	Saudi Arabia
South Africa	Brazil	Saudi Arabia	Russia	Poland	Iran	South Africa
Germany	Singapore	United States	Brazil	Canada	Indonesia	United Kingdom
Sweden	India	South Africa	Saudi Arabia	United States	India	United States
France	Indonesia	Germany	Mexico	United Kingdom	Saudi Arabia	Japan
Italy	Egypt	United Kingdom	Turkey		Egypt	India
Canada	Nigeria	Mexico	South Korea			Canada
United Kingdom	Mexico	Italy	Argentina			
United States	Russia	Poland	Chile			
	Saudi Arabia	Japan	France			
			Spain			
			Japan			

Source: Center for Creative Leadership. Adapted by Michael H. Hoppe, 2000. Not for reproduction or circulation without permission by CCL. Groupings of countries within each dimension convey greater similarity in cultural orientation.

Note: In general, greater proximity between countries conveys greater similarity in cultural orientation. Groupings of countries within each dimension, near the poles, or in the midrange, signal noticeable differences among these groups of countries.

through the subculture lens of gender, generational groupings, or ethnic identification, this prototype still dominates the popular and academic press. People with these characteristics are the heroes of the U.S. business press. Now look at Table 2.4. Note all the countries in the world where these are *not* the dominant values.

Cautions About Using the Cultural Dimensions Tool

Cultural dimensions represent societal-level prototypes of values and, as such, can be a very helpful or very dangerous tool for the manager with global responsibilities. Before illustrating how these cultural values might influence the expectations that employees, customers, or vendors may have about how a manager should behave, it is necessary to say a little about the use and misuse of this tool.

At some point in their lives most people talk about cultural differences even if they don't call them that. Sometimes cultural references are descriptive or humorous. Sometimes they are used to denigrate and devalue. Here is a very old European joke:

> *Heaven:* Where the English are the police, the Swiss are the bankers, the Germans are the mechanics, the French are the cooks, and the Italians are the lovers.

> *Hell:* Where the English are the cooks, the French are the mechanics, the Germans are the police, the Italians are the bankers, and the Swiss are the lovers.
> [From Hill, 1992, p. 17.]

People understand jokes like this—whether they interpret them as humorous or insulting—because such jokes represent a shared understanding of cultural stereotypes. Such jokes exist based on cultural stereotypes about people from every country, and the stereotypes are so commonplace that they are used in popular theater. Years ago when writing their musical *My Fair Lady*, Lerner and Lowe played on these stereotypes in the song "Why Can't the English." In it they lament the fact that the English don't teach their children how to speak and proceed to comment on the character of a number of different cultural groups, relying entirely on commonly held stereotypes.

Regional jokes within the United States are standard. How many times have you heard jokes about how slow people in the South are, how rude people in New York are, or how strange people in California are? These are all examples of jokes based in cultural stereotypes.

Most readers of this book will know their ancestry, and they will probably know how that culture is characterized or stereotyped. Garrison Keillor, the host of a popular U.S. radio show, makes people laugh every Saturday with his characterizations of Norwegians (as well as Unitarians, Lutherans, and liberals). His audience includes Unitarians, Lutherans, liberals, and Norwegians. They laugh at the jokes because they recognize themselves, their families, and their community.

When cultural prototypes are used as a tool, as a framework for understanding a country or a region, they can help managers anticipate how to behave when managing people from a different culture. A cultural prototype is simply a mental map that people can use to help them make sense of what is happening. The ability to anticipate, predict, categorize, and organize huge quantities of information is what allows you to process information efficiently. Cultural prototypes are a useful mental strategy for forming *provisional hypotheses* about what is going on or what is likely to be going on.

But cultural prototypes can cause problems when people forget that these prototypes represent the *average* person in a country, culture, or region and not every or any one individual from that cultural group. These mental maps *do not* and cannot adequately represent any single person. Prototypes are misused and evolve into prejudices when the description of difference becomes an evaluation of that difference.

But the use of cultural prototypes can be very helpful in making your way through a culturally complex world. Indrei Ratiu, a scholar at INSEAD (a world-renowned international business school) has claimed that successful internationalists know the cultural stereotypes of a region and use these stereotypes when first going into a country so as to have a provisional framework to hypothesize about what is going on (1983). If you can reach back in your memory, it is not dissimilar from asking a friend who has arranged a blind date for you for a quick description of your evening's partner. Your friend gives you an answer and you get ready for the date with a mental map or framework of what your date will be like.

Successful internationalists are able to let go of the prototype as they interact with people and get to know them as individuals. Returning to the blind-date analogy, as you get to know the person that you are with, it is likely that at some point you will say, "You're totally different from what I expected."

Unsuccessful internationalists either do not know about the dimensions on which countries, cultures, or regions may differ and so interpret everything from within their own cultural frameworks, or they never let go of the prototype in spite of what any individual might be doing to the contrary. As Nancy Adler notes, "In approaching cross-cultural situations, effective business people therefore *assume differences until similarity is proven* [original emphasis]. They recognize that *all behavior makes sense through the eyes of the person behaving and that logic and rationale are culturally relative*" (1997, p. 71, emphasis added).

Cultural prototypes are similar to the average numbers on the annual climate survey for your work group. You might receive data that tell you that the average employee in your work group is highly motivated and loves the job. But you would be mistaken if you thought that you had no motivation issues to deal with in your group. That average might be made up of twenty-five people who gave the group the highest possible score and another pocket of five people who gave the group the lowest possible score. The average climate score gives you a handle on what is going on at the macro level. Only by paying attention to the individuals in the group can you understand the complexity represented within that average.

Given this caveat, use Tables 2.3 and 2.4 as tools for understanding how culture will influence how the people you manage and work with may expect you to behave. Use them provisionally to form hypotheses about the behavior of others.

Applying the Tools

In the sections that follow we will illustrate how specifically to use these tools to adapt what you know—that is, the five essential managerial capabilities—to the global dimensions of distance, country infrastructure, and culture. In other words, we'll show you how to be the same but different.

Managing People When the Work Is Global

Just as there are different prototypes of cultures, cultures have different ideas about what a leader should be like. This can make being a leader in multiple cultures difficult. Even if you can figure out what each culture wants in a leader, how can you possibly fulfill those expectations? Some cultures don't even like the concept of "leader." One option is to find the commonalities among the cultures and then do your best with those commonalities.

Two U.S.-based theories of leadership make some claim to universality. A study by Bob House and 170 collaborators around the world identified twenty-two universally valued attributes of leaders. But they caution users of this research to keep in mind that these twenty-two attributes must be enacted in culturally appropriate ways.

Attributes of Leaders That Are Valued by Subordinates
in Fifty-Three Countries

1. *Positive*. Generally optimistic and confident.

2. *Encouraging*. Gives courage, confidence, or hope through reassuring and advising.

3. *Motive arouser*. Mobilizes and activates followers.

4. *Confidence builder.* Infuses others with confidence by showing confidence in them.

5. *Dynamic.* Highly involved, energetic, enthused, motivated.

6. *Motivational.* Stimulates others to put forth efforts above and beyond the call of duty and make personal sacrifices.

7. *Shows foresight.* Anticipates possible future events.

8. *Plans ahead.* Anticipates and prepares in advance.

9. *Informed.* Knowledgeable; aware of information.

10. *Communicative.* Communicates with others frequently.

11. *Team builder.* Is able to induce group members to work together.

12. *Coordinator.* Integrates and manages work of subordinates.

13. *Trustworthy.* Deserves trust, can be believed and relied upon to keep promises.

14. *Just.* Acts according to what is right or fair.

15. *Honest.* Speaks and acts truthfully.

16. *Administratively skilled.* Is able to plan, organize, coordinate, and control work of a large number (over seventy-five) of individuals.

17. *Win-win problem solver.* Is able to identify solutions that satisfy individuals with diverse and conflicting interests.

18. *Effective bargainer.* Is able to negotiate effectively and make transactions with others on favorable terms.

19. *Intelligent.* Smart; learns and understands easily.

20. *Decisive.* Makes decisions firmly and quickly.

21. *Excellence orientation.* Strives for excellence in performance of self and subordinates.

22. *Dependable.* Is reliable.

Source: Adapted from Den Hartog, House, Hanges, Ruiz-Quintanilla, & Dorfman, 1999. Used by permission.

Bernard Bass (1997) defines four leadership characteristics that he has found to be universal. These include exhibiting

- Idealized influence or charisma
- Inspirational motivation or vision
- Intellectual stimulation
- Individual consideration

But again, what is deemed charismatic, motivating, stimulating, or reflecting consideration will be defined through the lens of culture.

So whereas some aspects of managing and influencing people may be universal, it behooves global managers to know what others may expect of them because the dimensions of distance, country infrastructure, and culture will require them to enact even these universal attributes differently. Let us apply the tools of distance, country infrastructure, and culture to the example of Peter, something that a more informed Peter might have done before he decided to hold his videoconference call.

Please note that in Table 2.4 the United States and France have been marked on each of the seven dimensions. The position of the United States in the table represents the prototypical expectations of Peter and his colleagues and the position of France represents the prototypical expectations of the French. The United States is positioned among the dimensions as individualistic (source of identity), equal (source of authority), tough (means of achievement), dynamic (response to uncertainty), active (knowledge acquisition), scarce (response to time), and doing (response to natural and social environment). France is positioned as individualistic, unequal, stable, reflective, scarce, and being. (Table 2.3 provides a quick reference for the definition of each of these dimensions.)

We can then take each of the dimensions and form some hypotheses about how an American manager and a French manager might be expected to demonstrate leadership, one aspect of managing people. We can describe how each would attempt to influence, set direction, gain and maintain commitment, and mobilize a group facing challenges. We might hypothesize that an American manager skilled at playing the role of leader would be self-reliant, focused on work, pragmatic, and comfortable with ambiguity and action. This manager would not be expected to make much of the title, and would most likely set agendas and maintain commitment through a democratic and participatory process. The manager might seek the participation of others in setting direction and maintain commitment by rewarding individual achievement.

We might then hypothesize that the prototypical French manager would also be self-reliant. However, the French manager would place more emphasis on other aspects of life in addition to work, expect greater deference from direct reports as a result of holding a place in the organization earned through hard work and schooling, and be oriented toward a more reflective, theoretical, and predictive strategy for setting the agenda and facing challenges. Being right and accurate would take precedence over being opportunistic and first.

So Peter might be safe enough with his new French direct reports by acting as a strong individual, but he must also understand that the French are likely to defer to power associated with rank. Peter might be concerned about what he would consider undue attention to details on the part of his French direct reports. His French direct reports might be alarmed at Peter's action-oriented and tactical style. Given his state college credentials, they even might wonder if he is really smart enough for the job.

These are small and subtle evaluations that are felt but perhaps not even spoken to oneself. But such evaluations are pervasive and cumulative and they affect perceptions and behavior. If these judgments are not understood for what they are—misattributions and faulty evaluations based on unexamined cultural preferences and expectations—managers and their colleagues and direct reports in other countries will fail to make sense to one another. And in many cases they will fail to build the mutual respect and trust that are critical factors in working cross-culturally and at a distance. No matter how skillful Peter has been at playing the leader role in his own country, he must recognize that when he is attempting to influence his direct reports and colleagues in other countries, they will be expecting him to act differently.

Choosing to have this first meeting across distance compounds Peter's dilemma. Technology is an efficient shortcut best used by people who already know and trust each other. Refer back to Exhibit 2.1 (page 40). People who are working virtually across distance find it harder to establish trust and may have trouble establishing accurate perceptions of one another. This applies to people working within the same culture, and it gets worse with people who are from other cultures. On top of that, Peter and his direct reports have completely different beliefs about how he (and they) should behave toward one another.

The tools that represent the laws and business practices of a country are more likely to relate to those aspects of managing people that refer to the practices and policies associated with recruitment, selection, the role of the union, promotion, development, and appraisal, but you will be able to see how these practices are a reflection of the culture. Using Table 2.1 (page 44), note that the Latin European countries, which include France, are likely to have hierarchical government structures and that these governments are likely to be actively involved in industrial relations issues. In other words, Peter's involvement with union issues in France is likely to be highly scripted and determined by law from the beginning.

Compare this with the United States, which is closer to the British example in Table 2.1. Although there are laws determining union and management interactions, they vary from state to state and there is likely to be more latitude for an organization and union to work things out before the government gets involved. Country infrastructure is also likely to interact with how a manager might legally recruit, hire, and promote employees. Thus we might expect that Peter would find very strict laws in France governing how employees must be treated following a merger or acquisition, including a mandatory requirement to provide periodic career development and training to workers in danger of displacement.

Managing Action When the Work Is Global

For this example let us begin with the decision-making aspect of managing action. Please note that the United States and Mexico are marked in Table 2.4. This is a return to the example of John Smith from Chapter One. The dimensions of culture most likely to affect the decision-making process are the dimensions of individual-collective, equal-unequal, stable-dynamic, reflective-active, and scarce-plentiful. In using the framework we would hypothesize that the prototypical manager from Mexico would be quite concerned about the impact of a decision on his work group and company, would feel that it was his prerogative to represent and be responsible for this decision because of his place in the hierarchy, and would want to be sure he had all the facts and details before proceeding. Finally, we would hypothesize that the manager in Mexico would be less concerned with timeliness and deadlines than John Smith, who probably resides on the "scarce" side of the scarce-plentiful dimension. Above all, the Mexican manager would want to demonstrate his loyalty and concern for the well-being of his group, and this would be more important to him than saving a few pennies for the corporate offices in New York City.

While John Smith is in New York feeling a strong sense of urgency about resolving the problem of salary and cost of housing in Mexico, his counterpart in Mexico might be proceeding very carefully, wanting to be certain that when he announces his recommendation, he will have all the facts and that he will have fully represented what is best for "his people." If he is "wrong" he not only will lose face, he will have failed his group.

John Smith may conclude that this issue is not very important after all because his colleague in Mexico is taking so long to get back to him. His colleague in Mexico may think that this issue is not very important to John Smith because he is trying to rush to a solution.

Now consider these cultural issues within the framework of distance and virtual communication. Decisions that revolve around conflict are more difficult for people working virtually. John is in a hurry to resolve the problem but the culture and the medium dictate that it is going to take time to resolve. This issue warrants a plane trip for John even if it will add another $1,000 to the cost overruns. And John must gain a palpable understanding of the relationship of the Mexican manager to his work group. He was right when he said that this man was acting like a parent to his group members. He was wrong when he evaluated that negatively.

Finally, if we consider the dimension of country infrastructure, John would want to know whether there were country-based laws about housing allowances, indexing of salaries to inflation, and the tax implications of any decision he might make in each country.

Negotiation and conflict management represent the other major role under the general heading of managing action. Nancy Adler (1997) considers negotiation the single most important global business skill and maintains that global managers spend more than 50 percent of their time negotiating. In using Table 2.3 to hypothesize how culture affects negotiation, note that both the United States and Saudi Arabia are marked .

Imagine that a U.S. international human resource manager is trying to negotiate the adoption of a new set of HR policies and procedures with her Saudi counterpart who is at a slightly higher level in the Saudi operation than she is within the corporate HR structure in the United States. Gender is important here. Although the United States and Saudi Arabia are very similar to one another on the cultural values of doing-being and tough-tender, they are very different from one another on the individual-collective, equal-unequal, and dynamic-stable dimensions—dimensions that might be expected to play out when a manager must demonstrate skill in the role of negotiator and conflict manager.

The U.S. manager negotiating with a Saudi manager over an issue of potential conflict might hypothesize that saving face (not bringing shame on the group) will be critical to the Saudi manager. She should also be aware of the importance of hierarchy and status. In this case the U.S. representative is both female and lower in the hierarchy. Even though the responsibility for rolling out the new policies may have been completely delegated to her, in the eyes of the Saudi manager having to deal with someone lower in the hierarchy and female may be interpreted as insulting, mystifying, or peculiar. In addition, the U.S. manager may bring a certain orientation toward conflict to the negotiation; she may feel that it is good to get all the issues out on the table and grapple with them, versus the Saudi manager's orientation that conflict is best dealt with by discussing it indirectly.

There is a wonderful story about an Arab woman who serves apricots and spinach to her daughter's potential mother-in-law when she comes to tea. Because these foods don't belong together, the suitor's mother knows that these two people do not "belong together" and so the betrothal does not take place. There is no direct conflict and no loss of face.

Finally, as with the decision-making example, each party may bring a different time orientation to the table. The U.S. manager may feel a strong sense of urgency. The Saudi manager may have a much more cyclical orientation to the passage of time—and the circular and recurring nature of human conflicts. Although the U.S. manager may see the negotiation as short term (she will not have this assignment forever), the Saudi manager may view this interaction as the first step in the creation of a long-term relationship— that is, the nature of this negotiation with this person is the foundation for all future negotiations.

The role of distance in this example is self-evident and a review is perhaps unnecessary. Look at Exhibit 2.1 and note how distance would exacerbate these issues and how conflict and negotiation are best dealt with face to face. In a virtual environment trust is lower. Misattribution of motives is more likely. Entrenchment to one's own position is a significant concern. In issues of conflict and negotiation, trust must be established before the shortcut of technology can be employed.

Finally, it is very likely that the Saudi legal position may be very different from the U.S. legal position. The business sphere and the sphere of government are closely intertwined in Saudi Arabia, and the cultural set is hierarchical and unequal. There is unlikely to be a protest over any government-sanctioned, negotiated outcome. From the U.S. side of the equation, a protest is always a likely outcome. The relationship of the government to business practice is different, and the cultural value placed on equality will dictate worker response to a negotiated outcome.

Managing Information When the Work Is Global

How a manager manages information will be influenced by the cultural dimensions of equal-unequal and the norms associated with power, distance, and authority. And the expectations and demands of culture are likely to come into direct conflict with the outcomes associated with technology.

Look again at Exhibit 2.1. Virtual communication is characterized by greater sharing of information regardless of hierarchy and may lead to a more widely shared decision-making process. While this outcome might be acceptable to managers in a country that ranks high on the cultural dimension of equality, it would be less acceptable in countries that rank high on the cultural dimension of inequality. Imagine a global manager in Canada sending an e-mail message with an important announcement to his direct report in Egypt. To facilitate communication, he sends copies to all the Egyptian manager's direct reports. Now imagine his surprise when the Egyptian manager lets him know (most politely and indirectly) that the Egyptian manager was quite distressed by this action because it implied a lack of respect for the power of the Egyptian manager's position in the eyes of his direct reports. In this case knowledge is seen as power, and this power had been indiscriminately shared with everyone. It should have been his information to share. Another important component of sharing information that is most directly related to country infrastructure is language. Its use and its nuances will be covered more fully in Chapter Four.

Coping With Pressure When the Work Is Global

Coping with pressure takes on a different dimension for those working within a context of high global complexity. When people are working globally they are likely to encounter a great deal of unexpected behavior. People confronted with unexpected behavior from others will typically "jump back" from the strange event. This jump-back reaction is a healthy and normal response to possible danger from others, just as is pulling one's hand back from a hot stove. This jump-back response can be followed by a variety of other responses, but most commonly people will withdraw from the strangeness, attack if they feel threatened by the strangeness, or try to understand what they think is strange.

Managers who are very stressed are more likely to feel overwhelmed by the strangeness and will either withdraw or attack. Managers who are better able to cope with the stress of a global job will try to understand what seems to be strange. Managers with healthy strategies for coping with stress, confidence in their own ability, an understanding of the demands of distance and country infrastructure, and knowledge of how people from different cultures are likely to make sense of what is going on will make better choices. They will be more likely to want to learn more about what is going on and less likely to withdraw or attack.

A particularly charged reaction to difference was identified by Rajiv Narang and Devika Devaiah (2000) in a study conducted with culturally diverse, geographically distributed teams of software developers. They found that when dispersed multicultural teams were located in countries that had a historical colonial relationship, common miscommunications and misunderstandings such as those listed in Exhibit 2.1 were exacerbated and attributed to imperialistic attitudes and anticolonial reactivity. If planning was done at the home country and the home country was once the colonial power, and if implementation was delegated to a remote location and it was once the colony, then groups under stress reverted to the worst sort of cultural projections. To paraphrase Narang and Devaiah, team members at Euro-Asian sites adopted an adversarial attitude and team members at Asian sites adopted a passive defensive attitude.

In our frame, team members who are able to cope with stress and the confusion of difference and seek more information would be less likely to enter this cycle of negative attributions and recriminations. Using the tools in this chapter to make better predictions about how to manage across distance, country borders, and cultural expectations can become a stress-reduction tactic of its own.

Knowing the Core Business When the Work Is Global

Managers who were described as effective by their bosses and direct reports in high- and low-global-complexity jobs knew the business. To manage globally, they must now reassess their understanding of what customers want, what vendors can provide, and what the laws will allow in new markets and manufacturing sites. Adapting this capacity to the "same but different" framework is centered primarily on the country-borders dimension of global complexity because the conduct of business is determined by law. How to adapt this capacity will be discussed in greater detail in Chapter Three, because adapting one's knowledge to master the knowledge of international business is, in fact, one of the four pivotal capabilities.

3

What You Need to Know

The Pivotal Capabilities

Peter is obsessed by thoughts of his first encounter with his French team and is impatient for them to get back from vacation. He spends most evenings thinking about the unsatisfactory meeting he had with them. During the day he plans and replans how to get things off to a better start when they next meet. But instead of reading or watching TV in the evening before going to bed he replays that videoconference over and over in his mind. What should he have done differently? What did he miss? He certainly understands the business. He certainly knows the laws of France, and if he has questions he has one of the best legal departments in the world backing him. He decides that it was a mistake to have held the first meeting by videoconference, and he resolves to fly to Paris in early September to meet with the group in person. This makes him somewhat uncomfortable because he is not yet sure of his strategy.

The globe is spinning for Peter, and it has stopped in France. Peter is a very good manager in the context of the southeastern United States. He has had some minor problems with his people in Pennsylvania, but how is he going to do in France? Peter knows about business practice and the law. He is unlikely to make many legal errors. Peter knows about technology and he has read about culture. He knows these things in his head but he has never experienced them in his gut. He is especially uncomfortable with this "culture business" because in his heart he believes that people are people no matter where they live, and he believes it is wrong to stereotype others. He wants to take the time to know each person as an individual. Peter is what Judith Palmer (1988) calls a Paradigm I person. He believes that people are more similar than different.

If you will recall the tool about culture, Table 2.3, you will note that a belief in equality is very consistent with Peter's cultural frame of reference. However, it may be that at a level Peter is not even aware of, he takes viewing someone as different to mean they are not as valuable—not as equal. Peter has confused equality of opportunity, or existential equality, with sameness.

To become effective as a global manager working across the complex boundaries of distance, country, and culture, Peter will have to learn how to see the world through the eyes of others—or at least how to understand that what they are seeing is different from what he is seeing. He will have to allow his way of viewing the world to coexist with others' ways of viewing the world. To do this he will need the four pivotal capabilities—the axis that allows the globe to spin—mentioned in the introduction to Part I: international business knowledge, cultural adaptability, perspective-taking, and ability to play the role of innovator. In the sections that follow we will describe the four pivotal capabilities more fully.

The pivotal capabilities are specifically related to performance for managers in a global role. We put them in a separate category because unlike the five essential managerial capabilities (the "same but different" capabilities), our research indicated that the pivotal capabilities are critical to the manager when the work is global, but not when the work is domestic. These capabilities represent the knowledge and motivation to make the adaptations that are described in Chapter Two. In other words, to adapt the capabilities you have to a global context, you will need motivation, specialized knowledge, and a particular set of skills. The pivotal capabilities represent this mix.

To recap, the four pivotal capabilities are

- International business knowledge
- Cultural adaptability
- Perspective-taking
- Skill in the role of innovator

To help you understand exactly what these four capabilities mean, we list the knowledge and behaviors that make up each of these four pivotal capabilities in Exhibit 3.1. It might help you to refer to this table as you read the description of each capability. In Chapter Four we go into detail on how to acquire these pivotal capabilities. In this chapter we describe them and discuss why they are important.

International Business Knowledge

International business knowledge represents a solid understanding of business and how it is conducted in all the locations in which a manager's organization operates. If you will refer to Exhibit 3.1, you will see that this capability is an extension of the discussion about adapting one's business knowledge in Chapter Two. At the macro level, international business knowledge means that you have a thorough grasp of your core business and can see how to adapt and leverage that business within and across all the countries where you have markets, vendors, manufacturing operations, or natural resources. At a micro level, international business knowledge means that you know the laws, history, and customs in every country for which you are responsible.

To become an effective global manager there are experts a manager needs to talk with, classes to take, and books to read. A sophisticated grasp of international business not only informs the behavior of managers and helps keep them out of trouble, it also helps managers develop broad-range strategy and stay aware of how decisions made at one location affect outcomes and possibilities in

EXHIBIT 3.1. The Pivotal Capabilities.

International Business Knowledge

1. Creates innovative corporate culture to leverage unique, cultural-based knowledge and information for new product and service development.
2. Conducts cross-cultural negotiations effectively.
3. Makes deliberate choices about how to conduct business successfully in a given part of the world.
4. Applies knowledge of public regulatory framework in multiple countries.
5. Discerns and manages cultural influences on marketing and business practices.
6. Understands how culture influences the way people express disagreement.
7. Uses cultural differences as a source of strength for the organization.
8. Integrates local and global information for multisite decision making.
9. Negotiates effectively in different business environments, even with jet lag and through translation.

Cultural Adaptability

1. Evaluates the work of others in a culturally neutral way.
2. Selects and develops people in multiple cultural settings.
3. Inspires information sharing among individuals who do not know or see each other and who may represent different cultures.
4. Motivates multicultural teams effectively.
5. Adapts management style to meet cultural expectations.

Perspective-Taking

1. Listens well.
2. Takes into account people's concerns when trying to effect change.
3. Is able to view a situation through other people's eyes.
4. Recognizes the limits of own point of view.

Ability to Play the Role of Innovator

1. Forms novel associations and ideas that create new and different ways of solving problems.
2. Departs from accepted group norms of thinking and behaving when necessary.
3. Tries new approaches.
4. Is entrepreneurial; seizes new opportunities.
5. Generates new ideas.
6. Promotes an idea or vision; is persuasive.

---

another location. But intellectual knowledge is insufficient in and of itself, no matter how prestigious the business school where you earned your MBA. To know something intellectually is not the same as really understanding it deep down—being able to experience it, feel it, practice it. Do not be deceived into believing that because you have access to the legal department, the information technology group, and the international human resource division that you have all you need to perform at a high level as a global manager. If you cannot use this knowledge to alter your behavior appropriately for the environment and help others learn to do the same, then the intellectual knowledge is not useful.

That is why you cannot think of the four pivotal capabilities in isolation. These four capabilities represent an integrated package.

Cultural Adaptability

To be able to increase your knowledge and alter your behavior appropriately in response to cultural expectations you have to know what an appropriate alteration to your behavior would be. In Chapter Two we presented a number of tools that help describe cultural values, predispositions, and behavioral tendencies. These tools represent the knowledge of culture that you need to be able to adapt what you know, your style, and how you enact the various roles that a manager must play.

However, as with international business knowledge, an intellectual understanding of this information is just the beginning. What is really critical is developing and understanding the intellectual knowledge in a way that helps you act on the information. Cultural knowledge is a critical component of what we call *cultural adaptability*, the capability that will help you learn how to alter your behavior appropriately.

Cultural adaptability rests on the manager's ability to deal with the stress that the differences and "strangeness" will cause in a way that allows him or her to continue learning. In Chapter Two we briefly discussed people who can manage the jump-back response.

As we noted in Chapter Two, the jump-back response is caused by a complex set of feelings that managers may not even be completely aware of. They may know that something is bothering them, but they won't necessarily know what is bothering them or why. The jump-back response is related to that ill-defined sense of uncertainty that makes Peter feel uncomfortable when he asks a French manager for information and the manager gives him a thirty-minute answer or a twenty-five-page report when all he wanted was a quick response. It is part of what makes the U.S. managers laugh to mask their anxiety and concern about the formality and aloofness displayed by their French counterparts or the attention given their annual vacation. It is what makes John Smith uncertain about whether he should have hit the "send" button on his e-mail message to Mexico.

Using the tools in Chapter Two is a first step. These tools can help you understand what you are seeing and give you options to deal with the discomfort consciously. They help alert you to anticipate unfamiliar actions and motivations. The tools provide both a mental map and labels for what is happening. But general knowledge is not enough. Recall that Indrei Ratiu of INSEAD said that the successful internationalist starts with general knowledge and then moves to the level of the individual.

Perspective-Taking

When you are attempting to understand the point of view of a person in another culture, you must be able, at least intellectually, to hold the frame of that culture in mind as you try to see an issue through their eyes. The exercise in Chapter Two in which we identified the place of a country on the seven cultural dimensions and then hypothesized about how various management skills would be enacted is an attempt at perspective-taking—at holding someone else's frame of reference in mind. But you must also be able to experience the other's perspective.

There are several idioms that North Americans use to convey this capability of perspective-taking: *I know where you're coming from. I see what you mean. You have to walk a mile in someone else's shoes.* Perspective-taking is a type of empathy, and in the case of the global manager, it is really cultural empathy. Let us elaborate.

Everyone has a perspective. It is impossible if you are human and conscious not to have a perspective. To have a perspective is to hold an image or a belief about how something is or should be. To take the perspective of another is to be able to see their view of things, to understand how they think something is or should be.

Imagine that you and a friend are walking up a steep hill. Your friend is in better condition and therefore is about ten feet ahead of you up the slope. You both stop to catch your breath at the same time, so your friend is ten feet further up than you are. You and your friend both turn around to look back at the view. Your friend comments about the pretty town down in the valley. You turn around to look as well but you only see a wall of trees. Because you are standing in a different place, you see different things—literally. For either of you to see what the other is seeing, you have to go stand where the other person is standing. To get their "perspective," you have to see it from their point of view.

Walking up or down the hill to see the view through another's eyes is easy. Understanding how to act, communicate, or lead from the perspective of the deeply held values and beliefs of a colleague, customer, or direct report in another culture is *much* more difficult.

The actual processes and behaviors that represent perspective-taking are not complex or difficult to understand. They include the ability to listen well, the willingness to recognize that other people may see a situation differently than you do, the recognition that others hold assumptions different from yours about what is or should be, the willingness to solicit others' points of view, and the acceptance that your own point of view has limits.

This set of behaviors may not seem very "global." What manager has not heard of the importance of listening, soliciting others' opinions, and being respectful of differing opinions? What makes these behaviors unique to the global context is that when these behaviors are being enacted within one's own culture, everyone is working out of the same cultural frame. When a manager is attempting to apply these same techniques in another culture, the very frame of reference that each party holds about the world is different.

Learning how to understand another's perspective is easy for some people and difficult for others. How easy it is for you is an individual difference, but the skill can be learned. Just like doing math or playing the piano, it is easy for some people and difficult for others, but all can learn it if they are willing to work and study and try hard to be proficient.

Howard Gardner is a social scientist who has had a great deal of influence on expanding the commonly held views about intelligence. In his theory of multiple intelligence (1983), he speaks of six basic intelligences: linguistic, musical, logical-mathematical, spatial, bodily-kinesthetic, and personal. We believe that perspective-taking may be a form of personal intelligence.

Personal intelligence includes the ability to notice and make distinctions among other individuals and, in particular, to distinguish their moods, temperaments, motivations, and intentions. Unlike the other intelligences, however, "the varieties of personal intelligence prove much more distinctive, less comparable, perhaps even unknowable to someone from an alien society. . . . The 'natural course' of the personal intelligence is more attenuated than that of other forms, inasmuch as the particular symbolic and interpretive systems of each culture soon come to impose a decisive coloring on these latter forms of information processing" (Gardner, 1983, p. 240). In other words, perspective-taking is the ability to rise above your own cultural understanding of self and others and use your capacity for personal intelligence within the symbol system of another culture.

Another example of how fundamentally different perspectives can be was recently reported in the *New York Times* as the result of a study conducted with Japanese and American managers. Both sets of managers were asked to look at a picture and describe what they saw. The Americans described the individuals in the picture. The

Japanese described the setting. In other words, what was distinctive, what captured their attention, was different for the Japanese and the Americans. The Americans focused on the individual. The Japanese focused on the composition (Goode, 2000).

Perspective-taking is the ability to alter one's meaning structures. Individuals make sense of what they know within a network of values, beliefs, attitudes, and past experiences, and they interpret what happens to them through this framework. When they are working with individuals from other cultures, they encounter people behaving in ways that are incongruent with their own expectations of what they should be doing. To the extent that individuals interpret and label what others are doing through their own cognitive and interpersonal framework, they will make mistakes about others' motivations and they will respond incorrectly. They will make incorrect attributions about what they see. They will not *make sense* to others. To the extent that global managers are able to take the perspective of others, to learn and reorganize their own sense-making frameworks, their understanding will be transformed and they will begin to make sense.

Instead of jumping back or criticizing when something unexpected happens, managers with global responsibilities are able to use their knowledge of cultural frames and their ability to ask questions, listen, and test hypotheses to understand another's point of view. This is how Peter Dachler describes it:

> Global leadership has to do with knowledge processes, with issues that ask questions about how to deal with, understand, and accept multiple perspectives (rather than seeking one correct or true logic) and multiple voices (rather than warranting one authoritative, powerful, and most effective voice). In other words, global leadership addresses the urgent problem of how to understand and deal with being confronted with values, views, investments, and practices "not quite like us" in ways that we have never before experienced. . . .

Global leadership can be understood as raising questions about listening to and taking seriously other standpoints, generating mutual understanding, avoiding misunderstandings and "meaning vacuums" that lead to fundamental conflict, and building appreciation and tolerance as a basic requirement for realizing the potential of globalization [Dachler, 1999, p. 77].

Ability to Play the Role of Innovator

Glance at Exhibit 3.1 to see how we define *innovator*. A skilled innovator can try new things, create new associations, seize new opportunities, and persuade others to join in. Let's look at two examples in music. Depending on your age, consider the work of the Beatles or of Paul Simon. The Beatles went to India and discovered Ravi Shankar and the sitar. The music that resulted from this encounter was neither Eastern nor Western. It was altogether different. Paul Simon went to South Africa and discovered Ladysmith Black Mambazo. The subsequent music was more than the combination of American and South African sound.

In the global manager's world, the role of innovator is integral to the other three pivotal capabilities. If the capabilities of international business knowledge and cultural adaptability represent some combination of motivation and knowledge, and perspective-taking represents the ability to absorb that knowledge to a level of being able to experience the perspective of another, then the role of innovator represents the ability to take that knowledge and new perspective and not just tolerate, appreciate, or understand them but also to take two policies, procedures, products, services, or practices and create something new that is greater than the sum of its parts.

In some ways, this ability to create something new is the very essence of being an effective global manager. It is not just managing the context of globalization, it is leveraging it. But it is not a mystical or exotic talent. Skill at the role of innovator is the result of a step-by-step process of gathering information, learning to listen and pay attention, letting go of the need to be "right," and looking for useful combinations.

Let us return here to John Smith. Recall that John Smith was being hounded because of expenses associated with the expatriate program. When he explored the reason for the costs, he found that many of these unbudgeted cost overruns were associated with unanticipated and frequent trips back home by either the expatriates or their families. Most of the people returning frequently were Saudi Arabian nationals. He also learned that many of the spouses were returning to their home country because they found life in the host country to be hostile and strange. This early return by spouses became a reason for the expatriates to end their foreign assignments ahead of the scheduled time for completion.

John's first impulse was to issue a statement forbidding more than a certain number of trips back home and to make the consequences associated with early termination of an expatriate assignment more severe. After all, the Saudis valued the power associated with hierarchy.

Upon reflection, John recalled that Middle-Eastern values also include the notion of an extended family—people bound together in mutual support across generations and a variety of kin and friendship relationships. The reduction in the consistency of contact with these extended family connections was particularly profound for this group of expatriates and their families, so they traveled home more often than most.

John decided to fly to Saudi Arabia and meet with some of the repatriated spouses to talk with them and see what the issue was from their point of view. Of course, he had to honor the local culture and work through elaborate channels to arrange the meeting with the spouses. After a week-long series of meetings, John and the repatriated spouses came up with a new solution. John would work with the information technology group to establish a videoconference capability for use by families on a weekly basis from the office in Saudi Arabia and the offices of the cities where the expatriates and their families were located. The families of the expatriates were so appreciative of this acknowledgment of their needs and customs that unbudgeted travel expenses dropped to zero during the first year this benefit was offered, and the cost of the videoconference activity was less than 1 percent of what the travel costs had been. John could have ignored the problem. John could have issued an edict. Instead, John met with those who had a different point of view and together they created a new and innovative approach. This same example can be applied to the creation of new products, policies, procedures, and services.

One of our colleagues told of a British manager attempting to set up a manufacturing site in Africa. The area was very poor, so the manager decided to serve lunch and dinner at the plant as a way of recruiting a reliable and loyal workforce. However, absenteeism remained a major and costly problem. At this point the manager could have reminded himself that in many African cultures work is less central to life, and he might have reconciled himself to reengineering the work so that it could be accomplished by a constantly changing workforce.

However, the manager also knew about the cultural value placed on the well-being of the group, so he decided to spend time talking with the tribal leaders of the workforce to understand the problem (perspective-taking). The manager learned that the men were unwilling to leave their families hungry while they came to the factory for food. In a very unorthodox initiative, the manager began serving a midday meal to workers and their families six days a week. Absenteeism all but disappeared.

Ethics in Global Management

Though adaptability is a critical component of being an effective global manager, adapting your management style and business practices to fit the expectations of a particular culture and the legal and political infrastructure of another country introduces a relativity into the picture that makes most managers very uncomfortable.

Most managers have learned skills and behaviors that they believe are the "best" way of doing something. The relativity introduced by the global dimensions of distance, country infrastructure, and culture is discomfiting to most.

How should a manager from the United States respond when he sees an ad in a European newspaper placed by his company for a position specifying "wanted—ambitious young man under the age of forty"? What is the proper response for a strict Moslem attending a business gathering in London where alcohol is served? How should a Frenchman respond in China when he realizes his company's low bid on a project is being passed over for a bid from the principal's family member? What is a Mexican manager to do when his boss in New York tells him to stop thinking of himself as being responsible for his employees? Should a Swedish company send a female as an expatriate manager to Saudi Arabia?

Or consider the following, much more serious, example as recently reported by Norimitsu Onishi in a front-page story in the *New York Times* (2001). Consumers in Britain are trying to organize a boycott against the manufacturers of chocolate products (like Nestlé or Hershey). Legislators in the United States have passed a law calling for the voluntary labeling of cocoa-containing products to state the origin of the chocolate. These actions were in response to numerous reports over the past year that children are being kidnapped and enslaved on the Ivory Coast and sent to work in the cocoa plantations. Although Onishi reports that there are in fact very few children employed on these plantations and that all he met were sent there by their parents to help support the family, what he does report is equally disturbing when viewed through Western eyes. Child labor is the result of ancient customs, very large families, and profound poverty. The meager wages that the children receive for their work are based on local standards and the worldwide price of chocolate. What is the ethical response of a global manager in Hershey, Pennsylvania, when buying cocoa from an African, French, or Lebanese exporter who has obtained the cocoa from small farmers all over the Ivory Coast?

Global managers who strive to understand how others see the world, adapt their behavior accordingly, and work to use this understanding to develop innovative outcomes will eventually come face to face with an issue that represents what is, to them, a moral and ethical dilemma. When is something "right" or "wrong" versus simply another way of doing something?

We recommend two strategies for dealing with the ethical dilemma. The first is to encourage or demand that the organization develop (if it doesn't already have one) a code of conduct for managers to follow when working with and inside other countries. Managers should not have to make every decision alone and in isolation; the corporation should have some level of agreement about what is and is not an appropriate and acceptable adaptation to the customs and laws of another country.

One source of help is the Caux Round Table. As described in their mission statement on their Web page, the Caux Round Table is a group of senior business leaders from Europe, Japan, and North America who are committed to the promotion of principled business leaders. Started in 1986 by a few people because of a single trade issue that erupted between Europe and Japan, it has grown to incorporate distinguished and influential business leaders from many countries, including its cofounder, Fredrick J. Philips, former president of Philips Electronics; Kako Ryuzaburo, chairman emeritus of Canon, Inc.; and its current chairman, Winston R. Wallin, chairman emeritus of Medtronic, Inc. The members meet regularly, publish papers, conduct dialogues on substantive issues, and compile information about best practices to share with others. The Caux Round Table developed an international code of business ethics called "Principles for Business," and we have reprinted it in Appendix B.

A second strategy is to look at what the United Nations says. The U.N. statement of human rights (Appendix C) may help you in a variety of circumstances. This document, adopted by most of the countries of the world as a goal or template to strive for, may provide the reader with a more specific idea of how the world generally separates "ethical" behavior from "traditional" behavior.

This notion of relativity can be threatening but may also be the most powerful learning opportunity you will ever experience. A colleague from Brussels told us the following story. He and his family moved to a Pacific Rim country, where he had been sent to work for three years. When they got there they spent a few weeks traveling around and at one point caught a ship. The man, his wife, and their two children were hoping for a shower, so they hurried to their cabins. When they got there they found a toilet but no shower or bath. So the man went to someone on the ship and asked where the showers were. He was told that there were no showers, that there was just a communal bathing pool. If he and his family wanted to bathe, they would have to go to the communal bathing pool, strip off all of their clothes, wash themselves with soap standing by the side of the pool, and then jump in. Further, everyone had to go at once, and there was no separation by sex. The man and his family had to decide how much they wanted a bath, whether they were willing to go for three more days without one, and what they thought about being naked in front of all of those people.

What would you decide to do? How would you make the decision? What rules of behavior, beliefs, and expectations would play into your decision? There were dozens of men, women, and children together at the communal bathing pool. Would the fact that they didn't see anything wrong or strange in it affect your behavior? Think about it. It isn't a major moral dilemma like accepting an illegal bribe or stealing money, but it is something small that is related to many cultures' ideas about modesty, separation of the sexes, what children see of their parents, cleanliness, and so forth.

To tell you the ending (since it would be cruel not to), the family decided that it would be worse to go another three days without bathing than to bathe at the communal pool. They decided that they would let their eyes glaze over and not look at anyone (to preserve modesty), would not look at each other, and would bathe as quickly as they could. And they would not go back again—they would wait to get clean again after they left the ship. They lived through it and had a good story to tell. The man told us that what he learned from the experience is how his central beliefs about what is right are tied into his everyday behavior, and he learned where the line is that he won't cross with regard to ethical dilemmas. Though he found where his line was, he also found that he was more adaptable than he had ever thought he was.

However, this ability to adapt and change in response to the demands of the context also has some other consequences. Even though highly effective global managers may get high ratings for performance, they may also receive low ratings on being consistent and trustworthy. Highly cosmopolitan and adaptable managers may be accused of being "chameleons"—manipulative and inconsistent—by the people with whom they work, especially when the managers are of a different gender or ethnicity from the people doing the ratings.

Most people like consistency, and if you are good at adapting your behavior to the circumstances, many people will say that you are inconsistent. It is entirely possible that you are being consistent in the essence of what you are doing and saying (that you are saying exactly the same thing, just in a different way), but people may perceive the difference in delivery as difference in meaning. And that is the crux of the global challenge—understanding how the meaning is affected by the delivery for both the speaker and the listener.

PART TWO

Effective Global Management

It's Sunday evening and John Smith is going through his standard routine of packing his bags. This time he's off to Mexico and then on to England for an additional week. Armed with a laptop and a cell phone, John will never be more than a moment's notice away from his office in New York. Yet during the course of the next several weeks, he will cross fourteen time zones, hold meetings with his direct reports in Mexico, attempt to improve working relations between the Saudi plant manager and his employees in Britain, and address a variety of issues ranging from the devaluation of the Mexican peso to resistance to genetically engineered foods in Europe. Closing his suitcase, John laughs to himself as he thinks back to his days as a junior sales representative in Cleveland.

John Smith did not begin his career with the intent of becoming a global manager. He became a global manager as he progressed in his career and as his organization became global in its focus.

Like John Smith, many managers today are struggling to be effective across boundaries of physical distance, country infrastructures, and cultural expectations. While organizations have created advanced strategies and structures to be effective for global competition, they are much less advanced when it comes to developing individuals to be effective in global managerial roles. Nancy Adler sums up this point of view when she states, "The clear issue is that strategy is internationalizing faster than implementation and much faster than individual managers and executives themselves" (Adler & Bartholomew, 1992).

In writing this book, we make the assumption that you recognize the importance of developing managers for complex, global roles. Perhaps you are currently working globally and you desire to continue to develop within your current role. Perhaps you have aspirations to take on a job with global scope and you want to evaluate next steps you can take to better prepare you for this challenge. Or perhaps you are responsible for developing others who aspire to or already work in positions that are globally complex.

In Part Two of this book, we take an in-depth look at the dynamics of global managerial development.

4

What You Can Do

This chapter is about what managers can do to develop the four pivotal capabilities for global management: international business knowledge, cultural adaptability, perspective-taking, and ability to play the role of innovator.

We ask three questions: *What do you need to learn? Who are you? Where can you learn it?* Figure 4.1 positions these questions into a development framework that illustrates how the answers are connected.

What Figure 4.1 illustrates is that competence on each of the four pivotal capabilities is associated with at least two things. Competence (labeled "What do you need to learn?") is associated with

FIGURE 4.1. A Development Framework.

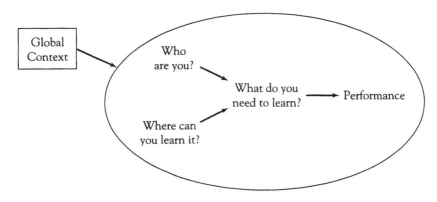

personality traits ("Who are you?"). It is also associated with international experience (labeled "Where can you learn it?"). In other words, people with certain personality traits and particular international experiences are more likely to have greater skill in the pivotal capabilities. (It is important to note that these connections are not causal. Our research is not yet that specific. We do not know that personality and experience cause a person to be good at something. What we do know is that personality and experience are associated with skill level. Where you find one element of the equation, you are likely to find the others.) In this chapter we explore what we think the relationships among competence, personality traits, and international experience mean and how you can use this information for your own development.

But first, we provide some background about how managers acquire the skills and perspectives necessary to become effective in their careers, whether their work is global or not.

Learning from Experience

Over the past fifteen years, the Center for Creative Leadership has conducted studies with practicing managers in organizations to understand more about how successful managers develop. Where did successful managers learn what they needed to know? How did they learn it? To answer such questions, these studies have been conducted by the Center several times (McCall, Lombardo, & Morrison, 1988; Dalton & Rogolsky, 1990; Douglas, forthcoming) and similar studies have also been conducted by other social scientists in universities and organizations (see McCauley & Brutus, 1998).

Our CCL studies focused on the following statement: "When you think about your career, certain events stand out as critical, things that have made a difference in your career, things that have made a difference in how you manage today. Please identify at least three of these events and tell us what these events were and what you learned from them" (McCall, Lombardo, & Morrison, 1988).

Managers told very similar stories in response to that question regardless of industry type, job function, or a host of other variables. They told the researchers that the most critical and meaningful events in their careers had involved either a challenging assignment or an important relationship. Managers also reported learning from hardships and training courses, but the bulk of the meaningful events were assignment or relationship based. Managers learned the skills that led to their effectiveness from the work itself.

Learning From Assignments

Examples of the kinds of assignments that managers identified as critical and important included fix-it assignments, start-up or green field assignments, an important project or task force, or a job with much greater scope and scale than they were used to. In addition, managers across organizations and functions reported learning similar kinds of lessons (skills, perspectives, capabilities) from these experiences. For example, managers in fix-it assignments learned the skill of interpersonal flexibility—being tough but fair while addressing a difficult issue. Managers in start-up assignments learned the skill of doing whatever it takes—forging ahead and getting others to commit and participate in an uncertain enterprise. Managers with task force assignments learned how to influence without authority. Managers who took a huge jump in scope or scale learned who to trust and how to delegate. Note that they learned these skills while getting the work done. Development was not associated with a solitary training event or the achievement of some arcane developmental goal within a complicated development plan to be addressed when the manager had time to think about it.

Learning From Relationships

Learning from others was usually about the manager's memories of time spent with a very good or very bad boss. From these very good or very bad bosses, managers learned about values and their impact.

And most important, managers recalled their very good bosses as role models—as exemplars or templates of a particular skill, capability, or perspective. For example, managers learned how to develop others, how to build a team representing diverse points of view and talents, how to manage a problem employee in a fair, just, and decisive manner, and how to work with peers across the organization to get work done.

These CCL studies have changed the way that the Center and HRD departments in many well-run organizations think about how to develop managers. What these studies suggest is that managers who aspire to a senior-level generalist job in an organization should seek out a variety of types of assignments in the course of their career and that they should try to work with those who are the best at what they do so that they can learn from them. Managers should be focused on getting the work done *and* on personal development in every experience that comes their way. Coursework is used to supplement experience—to provide skills training, content knowledge, self-awareness, or networking opportunities. But coursework is always used strategically and intentionally as part of experience-based learning.

We review this work because the same principles that support learning from experience in domestic jobs hold true for acquiring the skills and capabilities of the effective global manager. (We include additional sources at the end of the book for those who want to read more—see, for example, the Suggested Reading section for Dalton & Hollenbeck, 1996; Dalton, 1998; and McCauley, Moxley, & Van Velsor, 1998; and the References section for McCall, Lombardo, & Morrison, 1988.)

The following story illustrates this point:

Janet Bolton's family liked to travel, and so as a child she visited several foreign countries. As a college student she made this interest her own. She spent several summer vacations hitchhiking through the United Kingdom with her brother and her college roommate. After graduation she joined a company with production facilities located around the world. Because she had early success as a research and development engineer, she was assigned (based on her technical expertise) to headquarters as staff assistant to the vice president of operations for Asia. This vice president was an experienced international manager who could get along with people wherever he found himself. Janet traveled throughout Asia with him and had the opportunity to observe how skillfully he worked with people.

Her next assignment was as a production manager. There she learned through the grapevine about a new project team being formed to develop a quality-control process that could be used in manufacturing plants in Bangladesh, Alabama, Wales, and Malaysia. The team would be made up of people from all four participating countries. Because she had traveled in both the United Kingdom and Asia, Janet volunteered for the team.

Here the organization, in the person of a human resource staff member, made a developmental intervention. The HR specialist told Janet that in addition to achieving the team goal (designing a quality-control process that could be successfully implemented at all sites) she would also be expected to achieve an individual goal: learning how to be a more effective member of a cross-cultural team. So before joining the team, this young manager was assessed on such skills as active listening, acting with integrity, bringing out the best in others on the team, and demonstrating appreciation of cultural differences. She was asked to set developmental goals based on this assessment before joining the team and was encouraged to share her developmental goals with other team members. After the assignment, she was debriefed on the problems she faced, what she learned, how she learned it, and how the organization could use what she learned in forming cross-cultural project teams in the future. It was a positive experience for Janet, so she continued to look for international opportunities. Today this manager attributes her success to the fortunate happenstance of her love for travel, experience outside the country, a good role model with international experience, and an HR professional who showed her how to leverage the learning from her experiences [Dalton, 1998].

This story illustrates how managers learn critical skills and perspectives from experiences—specifically those in the form of assignments and other people. It also illustrates two additional points that are critical to development. First, learning from experience is not like sheep dipping. Simple immersion in an experience does not guarantee learning or at least learning the right things. Janet Bolton learned important interpersonal and intercultural skills from her task-force experience because she was focused on what she was trying to learn and she knew before she went on the assignment what she was trying to learn; the learning was reinforced because her team knew what she was working on. In addition, the organization demonstrated the value of the experience by debriefing the experience and using what Janet learned to inform the business. Second, Janet was probably drawn to this kind of learning, at least to some degree, because of her personality.

Other studies at the Center for Creative Leadership on learning from experience have demonstrated that adults have to work harder to learn some things than others. These studies have shown that it is important to understand who you are, because learning some skills may require you to go against the grain (to do some things that aren't easy for you). In other words, most managerial skills can be developed, but managers also have particular inborn talents and preferences. Managers can hope to become very good at some things and simply good enough at other things, but they can always improve their performance if they are intent on learning what they need to know.

How to Develop the Four Pivotal Capabilities

In this section we present, in three parts, a development framework for aspiring global managers. First, we focus on helping you develop a better idea of what you might need to learn. (*What do you need to learn?*) Second, we help you develop a better understanding of your personality and how it may help or hinder your development of different skills. (*Who are you?*) Third, we focus on helping you think about where you might learn what you need to know. (*Where can you learn it?*)

What Do You Need to Learn?

We assume that you, the reader, are already a reasonably good manager able to manage people, action, and information when you are working in your own country. You already possess a thorough knowledge of your business and your functional area of expertise, and you are reasonably hardy and able to cope with the pressures of daily life. In other words, you possess the five essential managerial skills that we presented in Chapter Two.

We invite you to test these assumptions by completing Exercise 4.1. This exercise asks you to rate yourself on each of the essential managerial capabilities. How well do you manage and lead when you are working in your own country? If you do not rate as well on this exercise as you would wish, you may want to concentrate on shoring up these basic skills within your own country as part of trying to adapt what you know for more global assignments. Some references for doing this are provided at the end of this book.

However, as stated earlier, it is the need to adapt your essential managerial capabilities to work across distance, country, and culture that requires you to develop the four pivotal capabilities for global management.

Exercise 4.2 is designed to help you answer the question, What do I need to learn? Please read each question and respond from the perspective of your boss, peers, and direct reports. If you are not sure how they might rate you, ask them. This may be an ideal time for you to take part in a 360-degree feedback experience that will give you some understanding of where you excel and where you need to develop. (The process called 360-degree feedback is a technique for getting information from your boss, peers, and direct reports about how they rate your effectiveness on a variety of skills. Such feedback is usually obtained by using a standardized survey, and the results are meant for your use, not the organization's. The ratings

EXERCISE 4.1. Do You Have the Core Capabilities for Managing in Your Own Country?

Please read each statement below and think about your performance over time *in your own country* as well as feedback you have received from bosses, peers, colleagues, or external stakeholders such as vendors, customers, and even competitors. Rate your level of skill from 1 to 5 using the following anchors. If your average score for any set of behaviors is 3 or greater, you might consider this as a core capability that you need to acquire. If you are not sure how others might rate you, ask them.

This statement describes

1. **One of my greatest strengths**
2. **Something I am good at**
3. **Something I can do but I need to improve a little**
4. **Something I can do but I need to improve a lot**
5. **Something I am really not able to do**

Ability to Manage People
LEADER

Am adept at establishing and conveying a sense of purpose within the organization. _____

Am a team builder; bring people together successfully around tasks. _____

Structure subordinates' work appropriately. _____

Recognize and reward people for their work. _____

Am effective at managing conflict. _____

Confront others skillfully. _____

Make good judgments about people. _____

Attract talented people. _____

Consider personalities when dealing with people. _____

Am a good coach, counselor, mentor; am patient with people as they learn. _____

Bring out the best in people. _____

Give subordinates appropriately challenging assignments and the opportunity to grow. _____

Make good use of people; don't exploit. _____

Am inspirational; help people to see the importance of what they are doing. _____

Am able to inspire, motivate people; spark others to take action. _____

Delegate effectively. _____

TOTAL divided by 16 _____

Ability to Manage Action
DECISION MAKER

Am action-oriented; press for immediate results. _____

Am decisive; don't procrastinate on decisions. _____

Am a troubleshooter; enjoy solving problems. _____

Can implement decisions, follow through, follow up well; am an expediter. _____

Can make decisions rapidly when speed and timing are paramount. _____

Can make good decisions under pressure with incomplete information. _____

(continued)

EXERCISE 4.1. Do You Have the Core Capabilities for Managing in Your Own Country? *continued.*

Ability to Manage Action, continued

Can modify plans in response to changing conditions. _____

Can create significant organizational change. _____

Can introduce needed change even in the face of opposition. _____

Manage the process of decision making effectively; know who to involve on what issue. _____

Am comfortable with the power of the managerial role. _____

TOTAL divided by 11 _____

NEGOTIATOR

Carefully weigh consequences of contemplated action. _____

Can organize and manage big, long-term projects; have good shepherding skills. _____

Can translate strategy into action over the long haul. _____

Build work and management systems that are self-monitoring and can be managed effectively by remote control. _____

Establish effective management practices for directing employees I see only twice a month. _____

Negotiate adeptly with individuals and groups over roles and resources. _____

Carry out negotiations with multiple risk factors and unknowns. _____

TOTAL divided by 7 _____

Ability to Manage Information

SPOKESPERSON

Am crisp, clear, articulate. _____

Am skillful in speaking to external agencies or
individuals. _____

Am a strong communicator. _____

Can effectively represent corporate interests at multiple levels
of interaction in public and private sectors. _____

Can effectively act as agent and advocate for the
organization. _____

Effectively represent the organization at social or civic
functions. _____

TOTAL divided by 6 _____

Ability to Cope with Pressure

Am capable, cool in high-pressure situations. _____

Can deal well with setbacks; resilient; bounce back from
failure, defeat. _____

Am optimistic; take the attitude that most problems can
be solved. _____

Use constructive outlets for tension and frustration. _____

TOTAL divided by 4 _____

(continued)

EXERCISE 4.1. Do You Have the Core Capabilities for Managing in Your Own Country? *continued.*

Core Business Knowledge

Am a good general manager. _____

Am effective in a job with a big scope. _____

Pick up knowledge and expertise easily in a new assignment. _____

Understand our business and how it works. _____

Understand cash flows, financial reports, corporate annual reports. _____

Tap local market knowledge and use it to underpin corporate strategy. _____

Am able to analyze and choose the best format for collaboration. _____

Know when and how to call on the specialized expertise of others. _____

TOTAL divided by 8 _____

Source: Copyright 360 BY DESIGN. Center for Creative Leadership, 2000. Used with permission.

provide you with some understanding of how you are perceived by others, your strengths and weaknesses; the information is not meant for appraisal, promotion, or salary purposes.) This 360-degree exercise should be designed to provide feedback about the four pivotal capabilities.

Look at your ratings (and the ratings of others) and decide which of the four pivotal capabilities you most need to develop. This should become your developmental goal. This goal should be something that you can imagine working on as part of the work that you do.

Think for a moment about Peter. If Peter were to first assess himself on the core capabilities from the perspective of his colleagues, direct reports, and bosses in his own country (Exercise 4.1), he would probably receive very high scores on his core business knowledge generally and as decision maker and negotiator, and he would probably receive better than average scores as spokesperson and leader and on his ability to cope with pressure. However, if he were to ask his new direct reports in France to rate him, he might expect to receive low scores on all of these core capabilities. To adapt what he knows and does well, he needs to gain new knowledge. He needs to recognize that people from different cultures have different expectations about how the world works. He needs to learn how his French colleagues conduct business, how they expect a manager to act, what importance work has in their lives. He needs to be able to work with them to create new possibilities and solutions. And because Peter is not particularly self-aware, he will need to start with an appreciation and understanding of his own personality.

Who Are You?

This question is an invitation for you to think about your personality and whether achieving your developmental goal will be difficult or easy. Your personality can be described by qualities that are typical of you and by the overall impression created in others in response to those typical qualities. In answer to the question, "What's so-and-so like?" we might describe a person's physical

EXERCISE 4.2. What Do You Need to Learn?
An Exercise Designed to Help You Assess Your Skill on the
Pivotal Capabilities.

Please read each statement below and think about your performance over time as well as feedback you have received from bosses, peers, colleagues, or external stakeholders such as vendors, customers, and even competitors. Rate your level of skill from 1 to 5
using the following anchors. If your average score for any set of
behaviors is 3 or greater, you might consider it as a pivotal capability that you need to acquire. If you are not sure how others see
you, ask them.

This statement describes

1. **One of my greatest strengths**
2. **Something I am good at**
3. **Something I can do but I need to improve a little**
4. **Something I can do but I need to improve a lot**
5. **Something I am really not able to do**

INTERNATIONAL BUSINESS KNOWLEDGE

Can integrate local and global information for multisite decision
making. _____

Discern and manage cultural influences on business practices and
marketing. _____

Can create innovative corporate culture to leverage unique
culturally based knowledge and information for new product
and service development. _____

Negotiate effectively in different business environments, even
with jet lag and through translation. _____

Discern and manage cultural influences on business
practices._____

Can apply knowledge of public regulatory framework in multiple countries. _____

Am able to make deliberate choices about how to conduct business successfully in a given part of the world. _____

TOTAL divided by 7 _____

CULTURAL ADAPTABILITY

Effectively select and develop people in multiple cultural settings. _____

Can evaluate the work of others in a culturally neutral way. _____

Can motivate multicultural teams effectively. _____

Can inspire information sharing among individuals who do not know or see each other and who may represent different cultures. _____

Can adapt management style to meet cultural expectations. _____

TOTAL divided by 5 _____

PERSPECTIVE-TAKING

Take into account people's concerns when trying to effect change. _____

Successfully view a situation through other people's eyes. _____

Recognize the limits of own point of view. _____

Listen well. _____

TOTAL divided by 4 _____

(continued)

EXERCISE 4.2. What Do You Need to Learn?
An Exercise Designed to Help You Assess Your Skill on the
Pivotal Capabilities, *continued.*

ABILITY TO PLAY THE ROLE OF INNOVATOR

Can form novel associations and ideas that create new and different
ways of solving problems. _____

Can depart from accepted group norms of thinking and behaving
when necessary. _____

Can try new approaches. _____

Am entrepreneurial; seize new opportunities. _____

Consistently generate new ideas. _____

Am good at promoting an idea or vision; persuading. _____

TOTAL divided by 6 _____

Source: Copyright 360 BY DESIGN. Center for Creative Leadership,
2000. Adapted and used with permission.

attributes (he's tall) or intellectual capabilities (she's smart), but we are more likely to respond with words that suggest attributes or qualities of a person that are consistent over time and situations. In other words, we describe people through the consistent impression they make on us: She's friendly. He's cynical. He's kind. She's a worry-wart. If someone in a given situation behaves out of character, people are likely to say things like, "That's not like him" or "She doesn't do that."

Personality does not refer to a single trait or attribute. Personality is a combination of traits made up of limitless possibilities of combinations and permutations that make us unique and allow us to know one another and distinguish one from the other through the unique patterns of our attitudes, motivations, emotions, attributes, values, and interpersonal style.

Although psychologists have long debated the role of personality in explaining human behavior, and have debated even longer about the stability of personality (how much people change or remain the same over a lifetime and how much of their essential nature was present at birth), the current best thinking in the field is that personality traits are part of the package we are born with and these traits help explain some of the things that happen to us throughout our lives.

Exercise 4.3 asks you to describe your own personality in answer to the second question, Who are you? Rate yourself on twenty-five word pairs that characterize you on five personality factors. These five factors represent what is called the *five-factor model of personality* and include

- *Emotions*. Your emotional response to stress.

- *Extraversion*. The degree to which you relish stimulation and being in charge.

- *Openness*. Your openness to new experiences and new ways of doing things.

- *Agreeableness*. Your level of interest in others and your concern for them.

- *Conscientiousness*. Your drive to work hard and achieve.

Research has shown that these five factors are more or less universal (Costa & McCrae, 1992; McCrae & Costa, 1997). They are found in people around the world. They are also found to be stable over the course of a lifetime. Even though people adapt and change over time as a result of everything that happens to them, some core of a person remains the same. These five factors represent this core. They can be thought of as an inclination to behave in a certain way. They predict when people will feel comfortable because they are able to "be themselves."

Returning to the example of Peter, when people speak about Peter's inclination to be somewhat quiet, they are probably speaking of a characteristic of Peter's that has been with him since birth. In other words, referring to the five-factor framework, his Extraversion scores would be low. This means that Peter might have great ideas but he could have trouble selling them to others. We might also suspect that Peter would have a very high Conscientiousness score and a relatively low Openness score. This would suggest that while Peter might be highly motivated to acquire all the new knowledge that is inherent in the pivotal capabilities of cultural adaptability and international business knowledge, he might have a great deal of difficulty discovering novel solutions in collaboration with his new French colleagues.

There is interesting background material that describes the relationship between these personality traits and managerial work. Three of the five traits are related to managerial job performance in many studies conducted in the United States and Europe (Barrick & Mount, 1991; Salgado, 1997). A moderate to low Emotions score is related to strong managerial performance. A relatively high score on the Extraversion dimension is related to strong managerial performance, and a relatively high score on the work ethic scale (Conscientiousness) is related to strong managerial effectiveness.

EXERCISE 4.3. Who Are You? An Exercise to Rate Your Own Personality Traits.

BIG FIVE PERSONALITY TRAITS LOCATOR

On each numerical scale that follows, indicate which point is generally more descriptive of you. If the two terms are equally descriptive, mark the midpoint.

1.	Eager	5	4	3	2	1	Calm
2.	Prefer Being with Other People	5	4	3	2	1	Prefer Being Alone
3.	A Dreamer	5	4	3	2	1	No-Nonsense
4.	Courteous	5	4	3	2	1	Abrupt
5.	Neat	5	4	3	2	1	Messy
6.	Cautious	5	4	3	2	1	Confident
7.	Optimistic	5	4	3	2	1	Pessimistic
8.	Theoretical	5	4	3	2	1	Practical
9.	Generous	5	4	3	2	1	Selfish
10.	Decisive	5	4	3	2	1	Open-ended
11.	Discouraged	5	4	3	2	1	Upbeat
12.	Exhibitionist	5	4	3	2	1	Private
13.	Follow Imagination	5	4	3	2	1	Follow Authority
14.	Warm	5	4	3	2	1	Cold
15.	Stay Focused	5	4	3	2	1	Easily Distracted

(continued)

EXERCISE 4.3. Who Are You? An Exercise to Rate Your Own Personality Traits, *continued*.

16.	Easily Embarrassed	5	4	3	2	1	Don't Give a Darn
17.	Outgoing	5	4	3	2	1	Cool
18.	Seek Novelty	5	4	3	2	1	Seek Routine
19.	Team Player	5	4	3	2	1	Independent
20.	Have a Preference for Order	5	4	3	2	1	Comfortable with Chaos
21.	Distractible	5	4	3	2	1	Unflappable
22.	Conversational	5	4	3	2	1	Thoughtful
23.	Comfortable with Ambiguity	5	4	3	2	1	Prefer Things Clear-Cut
24.	Trusting	5	4	3	2	1	Skeptical
25.	On Time	5	4	3	2	1	Procrastinate

EMOT = _____   E = _____   O = _____

A = _____   C = _____

SCORING INSTRUCTIONS:

1. Find the sum of the circled numbers on the first row of each of the five "paragraphs" or five-line groupings (Row 1 + Row 6 + Row 11 + Row 16 + Row 21 = _____). This is your raw score for Emotions. Circle the number in the EMOT: column of the Score Conversion Form that corresponds to this raw score.

2. Find the sum of the circled numbers on the second row of each of the five-line groupings (Row 2 + Row 7 + Row 12 + Row 17 + Row 22 = _____). This is your raw score for Extraversion. Circle the number in the EXTRA: column of the Score Conversion Form that corresponds to this raw score.

3. Find the sum of the circled numbers on the third row of each of the five-line groupings (Row 3 + Row 8 + Row 13 + Row 18 + Row 23 = _____). This is your raw score for Openness. Circle the number in the OPEN: column of the Score Conversion Form that corresponds to this raw score.

4. Find the sum of the circled numbers on the fourth row of each of the five-line groupings (Row 4 + Row 9 + Row 14 + Row 19 + Row 24 = _____). This is your raw score for Agreeableness. Circle the number in the AGREE: column of the Score Conversion Form that corresponds to this raw score.

5. Find the sum of the circled numbers on the fifth row of each of the five-line groupings. (Row 5 + Row 10 + Row 15 + Row 20 + Row 25 = _____). This is your raw score for Conscientiousness. Circle the number in the CONSC: column of the Score Conversion Form that corresponds to this raw score.

6. Find the number in the far right or far left column that is parallel to your circled raw score. Enter this norm score in the box at the bottom of the appropriate column.

7. Transfer your norm score to the appropriate box on the Feedback Form.

(continued)

EXERCISE 4.3. Who Are You? An Exercise to Rate Your Own Personality Traits, *continued.*

SCORE CONVERSION FORM

NORM SCORE:	NEGAT. EMOT:	EXTRA:	OPEN:	AGREE:	CONSC:	NORM SCORE:
80			25			80
78	22					78
76			24			76
74			23			74
	21					
72		25		25		72
70	20	24	22			70
					25	
68				24		68
		23	21		24	
66	19					66
		22		23	23	
64			20			64
					22	
62	18	21	19	22		62
					21	
60		20			20	60
	17		18	21		
58		19				58
56			17			56
	16	18		20	19	
54			16			54
	15			19		
52		17			18	52
50		16	15	18	17	50
48	14	15			16	48
			14	17		
46		14			15	46
			13			

NORM SCORE:	NEGAT. EMOT:	EXTRA:	OPEN:	AGREE:	CONSC:	NORM SCORE:
44	13			16	14	44
		13				
42			12			42
				15	13	
40	12	12	11			40
38				14	12	38
		11	10			
36	11					36
		10		13	11	
34			9			34
	10	9			10	
32				12		32
			8			
30		8			9	30
	9			11		
28		7	7		8	28
				10		
26		6			7	26
	8		6			
24				9	6	24
		5				
22			5		5	22
	7					
20				8		20
ENTER NORM SCORES HERE:	EMOT =	E =	O =	A =	C =	

(continued)

EXERCISE 4.3. Who Are You? An Exercise to Rate Your Own Personality Traits, *continued*.

FEEDBACK FORM

POSITIVE EMOTIONS				NEGATIVE EMOTIONS
secure				excitable
unflappable	*Resilient*	*Responsive*	*Reactive*	worrying
rational				reactive
unresponsive	35	45 55	65	high strung
guilt-free				alert

LOW EXTRAVERSION				HIGH EXTRAVERSION
private				assertive
independent	*Introvert*	*Ambivert*	*Extravert*	sociable
works alone				warm
reserved	35	45 55	65	optimistic
hard to read				talkative

LOW OPENNESS				HIGH OPENNESS
practical				broad interests
conservative	*Preserver*	*Moderate*	*Explorer*	liberal
depth of				curious
knowledge	35	45 55	65	impractical
efficient				likes novelty
expert				

LOW AGREEABLENESS				HIGH AGREEABLENESS
skeptical				trusting
questioning	*Challenger*	*Negotiator*	*Adapter*	humble
tough				altruistic
	35	45 55	65	
aggressive				team player
self-interest				conflict averse
				frank

LOW CONSCIENTIOUSNESS				HIGH CONSCIENTIOUSNESS
spontaneous				dependable
fun loving	*Flexible*	*Balanced*	*Focused*	organized
experimental				disciplined
	35	45 55	65	
unorganized				cautious
				stubborn

Source: Adapted with permission from Howard, Medina, and Howard (1996), CentACS, Charlotte, NC. This material is used by permission of John Wiley & Sons, Inc.

Note: Norms based on a sample of 161 forms completed in 1993 and 1994.

Caution: The profile on this form, which is derived from the Big Five Locator, is intended for use only as a quick assessment. Care should be taken to follow up this profile with a more reliable instrument, such as the *NEO-FFI* or the *NEO-PI-R*. See Costa and McCrae (1992).

In other words, some portion of the effectiveness of managers can be explained simply by understanding who they are. There is also work that shows that a high score on Openness is related to innovative problem solving and a high score on Agreeableness is related to the ability to be a transformational leader (Judge & Bono, 2000). Finally, a study recently conducted in the United States shows that childhood measures of intellectual ability, extraversion, emotional stability, and conscientiousness predict career success as an adult (Judge, Higgins, Thoresen, & Barrick, 1999).

However, when the manager's work becomes more global, these traits take on a different relationship to managerial performance. Although medium-to-low scores on Emotions and higher scores on the Conscientiousness scale are still related to performance no matter how globally complex the work is, of greater interest to those who want to become more effective global managers is the relationship of these five traits to the pivotal capabilities. In other words, the traits of Agreeableness, Openness, and Extraversion are not directly related to performance for managers with global jobs. Instead, these traits are related to the pivotal skills for global management. Now that you have completed Exercise 4.3 and have some understanding of your own personality traits, we will discuss the relationships between personality and each of the pivotal capabilities.

International Business Knowledge, Conscientiousness, and Emotions. Turn to your own scores on the pivotal capability of international business knowledge (Exercise 4.2) and your scores on two of the personality traits, Conscientiousness and Emotions (Exercise 4.3). Managers with high scores on this capability (an extension of the core business knowledge necessary for conducting business in one's own country) are more likely also to have the personality trait of Conscientiousness. This would suggest that those inclined to achieve, buckle down, and learn what they need to know (including taking some courses and doing their homework) are more inclined to have this specialized knowledge.

The connection between skills associated with international business knowledge and the trait of Emotions has more to do with managers' comfort in knowing that they do not know how to do something in another culture and their willingness to acknowledge their ignorance and learn. What is described as the arrogance of a manager working in another culture may actually be a combination of ignorance and fear. Managers who have gotten far enough into the hierarchy to have global responsibility often think of themselves as knowing what they need to know. They may also think that it is critical that they always appear to know what to do and how to do it. Managers who have a healthy degree of self-confidence, however, and are not given to worrying or having significant concern about situations are more comfortable learning what they need to know when they bump up against the unfamiliar. Managers who lack confidence may fail to learn because they don't know they don't know, don't allow themselves not to know, or think they have to conceal what they don't know. They may be very aware of their ignorance but also ashamed or embarrassed about it, so they try to keep it from others. If they are more invested in hiding their ignorance than in learning, they can't learn.

Cultural Adaptability, Conscientiousness, and Emotions. Look at your scores on the capability of Cultural Adaptability (Exercise 4.2) and again at your scores on the personality traits of Conscientiousness and Emotions (Exercise 4.3). Individuals with a low to medium Emotions score will be more likely to be able and willing to adapt their managerial activities to the cultural expectations of the workplace. Managers who have a lower Emotions score have a greater tendency to remain calm, even-tempered, and relaxed when presented with cultural differences. Rather than react sharply to these differences by jumping back, managers with low Emotions scores are more apt to stay in the moment and continue to learn.

The relationship between cultural adaptability and high Conscientiousness scores follows the same logic as the connection between international business knowledge and Conscientiousness.

Managers who fit this profile are more likely to have the discipline and determination to learn about cultural differences. They will be more likely to do what it takes to learn in detail about differences in customs, history, politics, and religion. When high Conscientiousness is coupled with lower scores on Emotions, managers will be more likely to be comfortable with the relativity of what they know.

Perspective-Taking and Agreeableness. Please note your own scores on the capability of perspective-taking and the personality trait of Agreeableness. Individuals who have high scores on the trait Agreeableness are more likely to be good at perspective-taking. This stands to reason because people with high scores on Agreeableness are described as being genuinely drawn to others and concerned for the welfare of others. People with these inclinations will be more likely to have developed the skill to listen to others. People who are more empathetic will find it easier to understand another's point of view. And those who are less inclined to be hard-headed and cynical (a description of people with a low score on Agreeableness) will be more amenable to changing their mind from time to time.

Think again about Peter. Certainly Peter's Louisiana colleagues trust him because he is like them—a local boy who has worked hard, knows the business, and can be trusted to do what he says he will do without wasting a lot of time. But does this mean he listens well, sees things through others' eyes, is truly empathetic to their concerns? Probably not. Peter probably has a low Agreeableness score. He is tough but fair, skeptical, and questioning.

Does this mean that if Peter's inclinations fall at the low Agreeableness end of the bar in Exercise 4.3 he can never learn to take the perspective of others? No, it does not mean that. It means that he will have to work harder than others with high Agreeableness scores to be able to learn perspective-taking. Taking the perspective of others, a pivotal capability in being able to adapt managerial behavior to the demands of culture and distance, will take real effort on Peter's part because his inclination is to be more suspicious, less trusting, and less concerned about the welfare of others. These are perfectly normal human traits, but people with these traits find it harder to see the world through the eyes of others.

Ability to Play the Role of Innovator, Openness, and Extraversion. Finally, look at your scores on the pivotal capability of ability to play the role of innovator (Exercise 4.2) and the traits of Openness and Extraversion (Exercise 4.3). People with higher scores on Openness and Extraversion are more likely to have the capability to play the role of innovator.

A manager whose inclination is to be more pragmatic, concrete, narrowly focused, tradition bound, and conservative is going to find it difficult to take on the role of innovator, so that manager is in danger of not translating the current skill set from "same" to "different" (see Chapter One). That manager may even be at risk of hanging on to the "one true way" and thinking that other ways are "wrong." Even when managers' inclination is to be very open to the abstract and the unexpected, if they cannot influence others to consider a new synthesis they have formulated (Extraversion), then the use of their skill playing the role of innovator will be limited.

A key challenge in determining whether Peter will ultimately be successful or not in a global role centers on his ability to create an open and trusting environment in which his American and French direct reports can collaborate. In his efforts to this point, we see Peter continuing to struggle in this capacity. His low Openness scores make him less receptive to the opinions of his direct reports. Having to address these new and different points of view is simply not an enjoyable experience for Peter.

A further challenge is that it goes against Peter's nature to want to be out in front, assertive, outgoing, and in charge. Peter will have to exert a measure of influence to bring these two groups together. Though he understands that this is what the situation calls for and he resolves to do better, his low Extraversion scores make this difficult. Again, do low scores on the bars for Openness and Extraversion in Exercise 4.3 suggest that Peter will not be able to get better at playing the role of innovator? No. But it does mean that it will take more work for him to learn this capability.

In the end, *all* the pivotal capabilities can be learned. They are simply a set of behaviors that a manager can acquire through some combination of feedback, modeling, and practice. Understanding *who you are* as part of acquiring these new capabilities is a tactic to help you prepare for demonstrating behaviors that may feel very much like they are against your grain. If you are prepared for the fact that you may be disinclined to learn something or you may find a particular approach unnatural, it will be easier for you to persist because you can steel yourself ahead of time. This personality data should help you understand what has perhaps kept you from participating in particular kinds of experiences in the first place.

This section of the chapter and Exercises 4.2 and 4.3 should have given you some indication of how to answer the question of *Who are you?* and why it is important. In the next section we will discuss how to integrate that knowledge with what you need to know and what you can do about it.

Where Can You Learn It?

Just as your skills and capabilities as a manager are related in some degree to your personality, they are also related to the experiences you have had. This means that individuals who have had certain kinds of international experiences are also more likely to exhibit competence on the pivotal capabilities. In this next section we describe the connection between these international experiences and capabilities.

How Many Languages Can You Speak? There is a great deal of controversy and discussion in the United States about whether managers need to be able to speak the language of the countries where they work. Those who speak other languages say it is essential, and those who do not say it is unimportant. In addition, for global managers responsible for multiple countries, it is daunting to think about all the languages that they might have to master. Fortunately for managers in the United States, English is the language of business. However, this is a blessing that may also be a curse.

In our study we found that the more languages that managers spoke, the more likely it was that they would have high scores on the capabilities of cultural adaptability, international business knowledge, and ability to play the role of innovator—three of the four pivotal capabilities. There are, of course, many possible explanations for this. For example, people who speak more languages may have lived in more countries, traveled at a younger age, been expatriates, and so forth; each of these activities is also associated with competence in the pivotal capabilities. Nonetheless, it appears that there is some independent relationship between how many languages that managers can speak and their skill in the pivotal capabilities. In other words, language is not directly related to performance; it is related to the capabilities that are related to performance. Speaking more than one language predisposes a person to be more innovative, have greater business savvy, and adapt more readily to cultural expectations of the workplace.

To return to an earlier point, managers who have grown up in the United States, in particular, are much less likely to speak other languages than managers who have grown up in other parts of the world. In *The Tongue-Tied American*, U.S. Congressman Paul Simon (1980) writes about the unfortunate state of American foreign language capability and emphasizes the costs paid for it politically, economically, and culturally. This puts managers in the United States who aspire to global roles at a significant disadvantage. It is harder to learn languages as an adult. Managers from multinationals based in the United States might also be lulled into believing that language does not matter because in most countries English is the language of international business.

We take a strong stand here and say that managers who aspire to globally complex responsibilities must make an effort to learn at least one other language. Even if you never become skilled enough to speak the language, taking on the syntax that represents a different way of thinking about the world will improve your ability to adapt and will change the capabilities that you have in situations that you will face.

Imagine working with Japanese managers who are able to speak your language in addition to their own. One expatriate told us of a company where it took a full year before the American expatriate in charge of the operation (who spoke only English) discovered that there were always two sets of meetings around any topic. The first meeting was conducted in English where everyone agreed with the American manager's pronouncements. He left the meeting thinking he had reached consensus on a topic and that everything would proceed as agreed. What he did not know is that there was always a second meeting in which the first meeting was discussed by the Japanese managers in Japanese. It was in this second meeting where the decisions about what to do were really made.

Whatever Japanese this manager might have been able to acquire probably would not have enabled him to participate in the second meeting, but attempting to learn Japanese would have taught him that he must adapt how he managed people, action, and information to the situation at hand. The language training would have given him a much greater appreciation of the situation. Or perhaps if the manager had made an effort to show more respect for the host country by trying to learn the language, someone might have eventually mentioned the second meeting!

How Many Countries Have You Lived In? In our study, managers who had lived in a greater number of countries were more likely to have the pivotal capabilities of cultural adaptability and international business knowledge. If we expand this notion to include significant time spent in another country, not just riding through on a tour bus, it underscores the need for managers who want to assume global responsibilities to spend time in a variety of cultures.

There is probably some critical mass of international experience that allows a person to develop a basic expectation that some things will be different in every country and so develop a strategy to watch for them. All people eat, but experienced internationalists notice what they eat, who cooks it, where it comes from, how it is served, and how it is eaten. The same is true for managing globally. All managers lead, make decisions, and so forth, but how do they do it? Experienced managers know that the context will be different and they have learned to watch for the differences.

One global manager we have worked with makes it a practice to arrive in a foreign country at least one day in advance of any business meetings. She uses this time to "do as the locals do" by hitting the streets, interacting with merchants, tasting local delicacies, sitting in public squares, and using her senses fully to take in this incoming information. She remarks that this practice helps to orient her to the culture and its people, which in turn serves her well as she goes into her business meetings.

Depending on the baseline information you developed about yourself in the last section, if you need to become better at managing cross-culturally and more knowledgeable about international business, you should travel, develop strategies to pay attention while you are traveling, and look for opportunities in your career to live and work in another country.

Where Else Have You Worked? One of the mysteries in research on expatriates has been the frequent finding that being an expatriate has not appeared to be related to performance in subsequent expatriate jobs. As it turns out, the expatriate experience is like the other international experiences we have mentioned. Managers with expatriate experience are more likely to have the pivotal capabilities, and it is the pivotal capabilities that are related to performance. Managers who have had expatriate experience are far more likely to have the skills of international business knowledge and cultural adaptability. In other words, the experience in and of itself probably cues managers to the fact that things are done differently in different parts of the world. This understanding is sufficient for them to prepare themselves correctly for future assignments by asking: How is it done here? If Peter had traveled in France on business rather than on vacation, he might have been much more aware of the formality that often exists between managers and direct reports and the cultural value that balances a respect for organizational hierarchy with a belief in equality.

What Can You Do While Still Working in Your Own Country?
Finally, you can develop the pivotal capabilities by going out of your way to learn from particular kinds of experiences. Managing people in your own country who are of a different gender, ethnic group, religious affiliation, or national origin is one way to develop the capability to see the world through someone else's eyes. Other examples of international experiences (to name a few) include working on or managing a geographically distributed and cross-cultural project, working in headquarters in the international division, working for or with an experienced internationalist, hosting foreign visitors to your city, and reading the literature or history, or listening to the popular music of other countries.

It is quite enlightening, for example, to read fiction by an author from another culture, even in translation. If you are from a highly individualistic culture, it might take you several novels before you understand that what seems like a bad ending from your perspective (the heroine gives up an inappropriate lover so as not to bring shame on her family) is actually a good ending from the point of view of a collectivist culture. One of our colleagues always reads the fiction of another country rather than a guidebook before a trip to that country. She finds guidebooks unenlightening about local culture. When she reads fiction, she "gets it."

Another friend told us a story of how he learned to listen to Japanese music. When he was in college he went to a concert by a Japanese musician. The musician played a selection that to our friend sounded like nothing more than a lot of noise. There was no beat, no melody, no pattern that he could discern. He started trying to locate the exit to see how to get out without causing too much disturbance to those around him. However, the musician suddenly set aside his instrument and said, "Now, allow me to teach you how to hear the beat of Japanese music." He picked up a ruler and began to tap on the podium in what the audience finally heard as a rhythm. After repeating this sound half a dozen times, the musician led the audience in clapping along with this pattern. He then returned to playing. Now our friend could hear the beat. He stayed for the remainder of the concert, which he fully enjoyed. He even bought the CD.

In other words, even if you are not going to learn another language or do not have the opportunity to become an expatriate or serve on a culturally and geographically dispersed work group in the immediate future, you should be seeking out experiences that challenge your perspective and offer other perspectives. In most cities in most countries, you do not have to walk very far before you discover another culture in the form of a restaurant, a street corner, a neighborhood, a specialized bookstore. Pay attention!

Peter has accepted the fact that the situation in France is not going very well. During his first visit he found it difficult to connect with his new direct reports, and even though they spoke English to him and behaved in a very respectful manner, he never felt like he was really accepted. He was simply tolerated. He flew home determined to fix whatever was wrong. He acknowledged to his wife that he was at least part of the problem.

At his wife's suggestion, the first thing Peter did was to go and talk with an old friend of his who had once been an expatriate. This individual took him out to lunch and spent a long time telling him stories, funny in retrospect, about all the mistakes he had made when he was first assigned to work in Mexico. It did not matter that he was talking about another country, not France. He made the notion of culture come alive for Peter. Peter was able to see that countries really do have different cultures and that culture really matters.

The next thing that Peter did was get online and order some books about France. He ordered guidebooks and history books. He also subscribed to a daily online news service that provided him with a synopsis of international news and business stories. Significantly, the news service was European in origin. He found that he was able to scan the international news within only a few minutes each morning and it provided him with a better understanding of what was happening in the world. He also sent the link for this service to all his direct reports. He ordered some French language tapes to play in the car on his way to and from work, although he did have a hard time keeping focused on them. His mind would wander and he would have to hit the rewind over and over to catch what he had missed. He did not have much hope of learning French this way, but the syntax and the rhythm of the accent were starting to sound familiar to him.

And finally, Peter went to visit his HR manager. The HR manager gave Peter a copy of the personality test and the pivotal skills assessment that are provided in this chapter (Exercises 4.2 and 4.3). Peter took the personality test and he used the pivotal skills assessment as a 360-degree feedback so that he could see what his U.S. work group thought about his capabilities. He went ahead and asked his work group to rate him on the core capabilities as well so that he could see how he was doing in his own country with the basics.

Peter found that others described him as a pretty stable, conscientious, and hard-working manager, inclined to be quiet, a little suspicious and distant, pretty straightforward, and conventional in his intellectual approach to things. He also found out that while people thought he was doing a great job on the core capabilities, they did not see him as very culturally astute, or very good at seeing things from another's point of view. Nor did they see him as very innovative.

Peter decided to concentrate on acquiring the skills of perspective-taking and playing the role of innovator. He was not as worried about the other two pivotal skills because he knew he could learn what he needed to know in that arena. He was more concerned that even if he read everything he needed, he would not really "get it." His developmental goals were to become a better listener—especially with people he would have once dismissed as too far out. He also resolved to do a better job of asking people for their opinions and to demonstrate that he was listening to them, especially when he did not agree with them, by stating what they had said back to them for clarification before he countered with a different opinion. Much to his surprise, he soon found that he was countering with a different opinion much less frequently.

Since Peter was already in a new assignment, he did not need to seek out a developmental assignment that would challenge him to learn. He simply needed to leverage the assignment he already had.

He decided to enlist his French colleagues to help him become more culturally versatile. He had read that the French value intellectual ability, technical expertise, and an elegance of logic. Peter knew that he could hold his own with his knowledge of the industry and so he felt he could spend some of his "credit" as an expert to enlist their help in teaching him what the French expect from a manager. Although he felt a little nervous about making himself vulnerable (he did not want to appear weak), he knew of no other way to make sense of their expectations than to ask them for their help and feedback.

He tried this tactic on his next trip to France. When his French direct reports started to overwhelm him with the details of a project, he told them that he was really surprised that managers at this level would go into such detail and compared their practice to that of the United States. He told them that he would try to keep in mind that they would, therefore, expect a greater level of detail from him. Although a few eyebrows went up, his acknowledgment of their expectations was well received. He was judged as a person willing to learn, and it occurred to a few of his French direct reports that it would not be a bad thing for them to learn something about American expectations for their behavior.

Peter is becoming an effective global manager. Some things are especially hard for him, but by being alert and learning what he needs to know even when it doesn't come easily, he's beginning to develop the pivotal skills.

It Is Not Just About You

It is probably apparent to you that no single manager can expect to be good at all these skills. If you will think about the relationship of personality to managerial performance, you will note two things. First, you will note that some of the traits predict opposite outcomes. For example, Conscientiousness is highly related to managerial performance when the work is familiar and the problems are routine, but it is negatively related to performance when the work is unfamiliar and the problems require innovative solutions. The opposite is true of the trait Openness. Second, you will note that most people are unlikely to be high on all the personality traits of Agreeableness, Extraversion, Openness, Conscientiousness, and Emotions. Rather, most people will be high on some, average on some, and low on others. (And low is not bad. It just represents the other end of the spectrum.)

So, as a manager preparing for global responsibilities, not only should you be seeking out experiences to develop your own skills with the knowledge that some things will be easier to learn than others, you should also be identifying the talents, preferences, and inclinations of your peers, direct reports, and colleagues and making room for them to complement your skill set with their own. This will actually give you yet another opportunity to practice perspective-taking and innovation.

In the next chapter we will discuss what organizations can do to develop managers for global responsibilities. You may read Chapter Five from any one of three points of view. You may read the chapter for yourself. *What are the activities you need to participate in to develop your own skills?* You may read the chapter from your perspective as a manager. *What are the activities that you need to provide for those you supervise?* Or you may read the chapter from the perspective of a policymaker. *What are the policies, practices, and philosophies that you must set in place to ensure a ready stream of global management talent?*

5

What Your Organization Can Do

Organizations doing business in the global economy must have the management and leadership talent to address the work. Therefore, organizations need a well-defined plan for the development of managers able to work effectively in complex global environments.

A well-defined plan includes

- A recruitment strategy that targets both individuals with international experience and individuals with a demonstrated interest in learning from challenge and variety.

- An internal recruitment strategy that incorporates all the potential talent available from around the world.

- An assessment process that provides individuals with information about who they are and what they need to develop. This assessment process may also become an organizational culture tool used to seed the organization with an understanding of the knowledge and attitudes that are valued within the organization.

- The strategic and thoughtful use of experience as the most powerful development strategy available.

In Chapter Four we discussed what individuals can do to develop the knowledge and capabilities that will help them become more effective as they grapple with complex global managerial responsibilities. In this chapter we address the same set of issues from the organizational perspective. What are the systems and practices that can be put in place by HRD professionals and managers who are responsible for the development of others?

We organize the discussion around five topics: early identification, country-based glass ceilings, effectiveness in a global context, baseline information for employees about what is expected, and the strategic use of experience. The following seven questions will help you think through your organization's development strategy for global managers.

Designing a Process to Develop Global Managers:
Questions to Ask About Your Organization

- Are we recruiting people with international experience and people who speak at least one language in addition to their own?

- Are we recruiting people who demonstrate an interest in novelty, learning, and an interest in others?

- Does our internal talent pool reflect the brightest and best, wherever they are located, wherever they might be from?

- Is our development plan aligned with the organizational strategy?

- Do our target performance capabilities reflect the multiple facets of effectiveness?

- Do our employees know how they are doing and what they need to learn in order to advance their careers and the goals of the organization?

- Do we use people and assignments strategically to advance the goals of the organization and the careers of the individuals who make up the organization?

Early Identification

"Even in this day and age and even with Fortune 500 companies, it is difficult to convince recruiting departments and managers of the benefits of hiring a student with multicultural sensitivity, who is bilingual, who has international exposure and a real knowledge of international business over a person with a (traditional) MBA" (Feldman & Thompson, 1992, p. 361).

We do not mean to suggest that it is too late for your middle-level and executive managers to develop global knowledge and capability. They can develop these capabilities; but we also know that it won't happen overnight and that development is going to take some time. If you wish to institute a systemic approach to development, it is easiest and most efficient to start early and incorporate the global development initiative into your strategies for recruitment and individual development in addition to your strategies for management and executive development and succession.

Our own work and the work of others tells us that you should be looking for two elements when you recruit: international experience and willingness to learn. The international experience includes language capability, education abroad, international travel, experience living in another country, degrees in international subjects (business, history, political science, economics, or language), and even childhood experiences. These activities are related to cultural knowledge and they are related to the capabilities of perspective-taking and ability to play the role of innovator. Our research and the research of others tells us that people who have had these experiences, because of choice or the accident of birth, are more likely to become effective global managers.

However, it would be a bad idea to limit your recruitment strategies to these people. There are not enough of them, they are not all good at this work, and there are other people who have learned the same skills and capabilities in other venues. One of the best expatriate managers that we know grew up in a small town in the rural South, attended an in-state college, and had never been out of the country until he was sent on a business trip during his first year of employment as a chemist. When asked if there was anything in his life that had prepared him for an expatriate experience he told the interviewer that all of his life he had wanted to travel and learn about other places. He had no idea where that came from. His parents and grandparents had little spirit of adventure; his forebears had come from England in the late 1700s and their descendants had stayed put. His wanderlust seemed like an anomaly.

What this story illustrates is that in addition to hiring people with international backgrounds or a particular knowledge base, you also want to look for people who are open to learning, who enjoy novelty, and who relish difference. To identify these people you may have to change the nature of your interview strategy. You must move away from simply asking people to recite accomplishments or from looking at their grade-point average. You must ask them to compare and contrast; describe activities that were challenging and tell you what they learned from them; tell you about what they have discovered when they have worked, studied, and been roommates with people who were different.

Recall the adjectives that describe the traits of Agreeableness and Openness in Exercise 4.3. These are the characteristics that you are trying to unearth in your interview process. These are the characteristics that should appear somewhere on your high-potential checklist.

Breaking the Country-Based Glass Ceiling

Readers located in the United States will know the expression "glass ceiling" as a phrase describing implicit and explicit organizational strictures that prevent women and people of color from moving above a certain level in the organization. This same phenomenon exists in organizations that talk about being global but, in fact, have peopled the executive ranks only with nationals representing the country location of corporate headquarters.

Where this practice exists in an organization (and it seems to exist in most international organizations around the world), it results in people from other parts of the world feeling less valued. There are morale and retention problems in the management ranks of organizations throughout the world. The bottom line is that the best and brightest of your management talent is unlikely to remain with you if they know that they can never rise above the level of country manager. If they must watch an endless parade of expatriate managers from corporate headquarters who are being provided with the best developmental assignments, knowing that it is unlikely that such opportunities will ever come their way, they will go somewhere else. If they know that only those born in the country of corporate headquarters will ever make it to the executive committee, they may well fail to work as hard or be as dedicated. It is a waste of time to recruit the brightest and best if you intend to put a glass ceiling in their way. They will not stay with the organization, their leaving will send a negative message, and the result will be an organization that will never become truly globally effective.

Effectiveness in the Global Context: Setting the Target

Effectiveness is in the eye of the beholder. When an organization wants to develop effective managers, there must be some shared understanding of what effectiveness means. There must be agreement that a manager with certain skills and capabilities will be able to move the organization in the direction it needs to go—that skills and strategy are aligned. And those who are being asked to develop a new skill set must be able to see that colleagues who learn new things are rewarded.

Those of you familiar with multisource feedback techniques know that even when all a manager's raters are from the same country and co-located in the same city, that manager's effectiveness ratings are likely to vary substantially depending on the point of view of the boss, the peers, the direct reports, and the customers. It is the rare person who is seen as effective by bosses, colleagues, *and* direct reports.

When you are preparing managers to be effective in a globally complex job, you must multiply the perspectives of the various organizational levels by cultural expectations. If you will recall the examples of "same but different" in Chapter Two, it will be easy to imagine how cultural expectations influence perceptions of effectiveness and interact with the points of view of bosses, peers, and direct reports. For example, in many studies of expatriate effectiveness it is common to find that the home country boss will rate an expatriate manager highly for looking out for the best interests of "corporate"—while direct reports in the host country rate this same manager poorly for the same behavior. Conversely, an expatriate manager who is perceived by host country direct reports as concerned for their well-being and the well-being of the local division of the company makes headquarters uneasy.

In our work we found several factors that influenced global managers' performance ratings. These included

- *Hierarchical level*—boss and direct reports did not see eye to eye.
- *Country of origin*—when the boss or direct reports were from a different country than the manager, the ratings were lower.
- *Gender and race*—women and people of color received lower ratings from their bosses.
- *International experience*—people who were more culturally sophisticated were perceived to get along less well with peers.
- *Cultural region*—cultural regions use rating scales differently, so a 4 may mean very well done in one country and only better than average in another.

Each of these factors represents a lens, a filter through which a manager's work is judged—and the person working in a complex global environment is also often working virtually and from a distance.

So the first step in creating some shared understanding about what effectiveness means—the target that you are shooting for—is to be certain that this set of behaviors is one that will allow the manager working globally to be perceived as effective through these multiple lenses.

You must also take into account that different countries have different expectations about what an effective manager will be able to do. Recall from the discussion of effectiveness in Chapter One the description of Derr and Laurent's study on what makes an effective manager. Germans value technical creativity. Americans value entrepreneurs. French value the ability to manage power relationships. The framework for effectiveness that you develop for your company should be influenced both by your corporate culture and by the need to create a more global framework of effective management. In other words, managers who are evaluated as effective based on the standards of their own country also need to be able to adapt their behavior to be seen as effective by others with different expectations. The standard you set will not be that of either entrepreneur or creative technocrat. It will need to be the standard of moving the business forward through the innovative use of multiple perspectives and points of view.

Providing Employees with Baseline Information

The template of effective global managerial behaviors must be shared with the organization at large. Individuals should receive multisource feedback on a regular basis, and the feedback should be directly related to the template of effective global managerial behavior. Managers armed with this feedback should be encouraged to generate development plans such as those described in Chapter Four.

However, to create the capabilities that we advocate in this book, providing regular feedback also means that you are seeding the organization with a set of principles rather than just holding up a list of competencies. Remember that in a global organization, everyone has to keep the global perspective in mind even if they are not managing across the borders of distance, country, and culture.

Providing all managers with feedback on the global capabilities is a way to create a more globally aware organization. With this practice you are advocating that managers develop their capabilities within their own country, while at the same time reminding them that what they are learning is only going to be partially transferable to other places. It is of use in the context of their current job in their own country. You are advocating that managers start early in their careers to seek out challenges so that they are always learning. You are advocating that managers keep focusing on learning, long after they are out of university. They need to keep learning how business is done around the world and what that means to their work. You are advocating for a culture in which people learn to really listen and pay attention to one another— even if they strongly disagree. You are advocating for a culture in which innovation is encouraged, recognized, and rewarded. But this is not the innovation of the solitary inventor; this is innovation that leverages the differences that exist among people, cultures, and country systems.

Providing feedback to individuals about their level of proficiency on a set of capabilities must not deteriorate into a sterile measurement against a competency list. Rather, the pivotal capabilities should be used to suggest something dynamic, changing, and ongoing—the knowledge and attitudes of a manager working in a context of global complexity and constant change.

And to add to the complexity, be aware that multisource feedback will be perceived differently by managers and their raters within different cultural contexts. Although we are advocating this process as a way to let managers who aspire to global roles know where they stand and what they need to learn, we are also advocating that the procedure must be adapted to a given cultural context. Book chapters by Hoppe (1998) and by Leslie, Gryskiewicz, and Dalton (1998) address the use of multisource feedback in other countries.

Using People and Assignments Strategically

What do you do next? It is important to begin a system of development by being clear about the knowledge and behaviors you are trying to develop. We recommend that your target include knowledge of international business and cultural differences, along with the capabilities of perspective-taking and ability to play the role of innovator—that is, all the pivotal capabilities for global management. You recruit a pool of people who have some of the experiences and characteristics of the effective global manager. And then you go about teaching these recruits and the managers they work with how to learn from these experiences.

What this means is that you must seed the organization with the same kinds of information that was provided to individuals in Chapter Four. Your development pool must be provided with some baseline understanding of who they are, what they need to know, and where they can learn it.

These kinds of assessment, feedback, and information sharing activities are often event-based. Individuals are brought together in a group setting to receive feedback on their personality, skill level, and knowledge base, and they are told how to use this information to develop the ability to manage in complex global environments. Unfortunately, for many organizations this is where their developmental efforts stop. Event-based feedback, however powerful, compelling, and meaningful to individuals, is insufficient to drive an organizational strategy.

There must be a next step: developing an inventory of experiences that will provide people with the opportunity to learn what they need to know. This inventory includes experiences such as working with a diverse project team in one's own country, business trips abroad, membership on a virtual and multicountry project team, managing such a team, serving as an expatriate in an individual contributor role, serving as an expatriate in a managerial role, rolling out a new product or policy or service across country borders, working for an experienced and skilled international manager, and so on.

You are looking for opportunities where work needs to be done *and* where there is an opportunity to learn how to do this work across the borders of distance, country, and culture. You are also teaching the managers responsible for the development of others how to become aware of these responsibilities. You are seeking to develop an organizational culture in which each assignment or opportunity is considered a developmental assignment for someone. This does not mean that all assignments can be developmental. It does mean that every assignment should be weighed as an opportunity.

And then you have to teach your aspiring global managers and those responsible for developing them (their bosses) how to learn. What this means is that managers who are being given a developmental assignment need to know the following:

- How this experience is related to their career path
- How this experience is related to the needs of the business
- What they are expected to accomplish
- What they are expected to learn
- Who will serve as coach or role model
- Who will provide feedback
- How they will be held accountable for the task and the learning
- How to access coursework if it is needed
- How to employ a variety of tactics as part of the learning strategy
- The consequences of a failure to learn, if any

Those of you familiar with the history of Center for Creative Leadership research will say, "What is different here? This is about learning from experience. This is about being both planful and opportunistic. This is about sharing the responsibility and accountability for development among individuals, HR practitioners, senior executives, and line managers." And you will be correct. Just as Chapter Two was about managerial capabilities that were the same but different, designing developmental processes for managers who will need to manage across complex and multiple borders is also the same but different.

It is still true that managers learn much of what they need to know from the work itself. What is different about managing and leading globally is the pool you select from, the knowledge and capabilities that you seek to instill, and the experiences that you provide. What is different about the material presented in this book is that we have learned more about the links between personality and skill, and we have learned more about the kinds of experiences specifically related to the development of certain skills. The principles of learning from experience are the same. The methodologies you use to implement these principles must be accommodated to the culture in which you are working.

Organizations doing business in the global economy must have the management and leadership talent to address the work. "The CEO of a global company cannot change her message for each of the countries and cultures in which her company operates. . . . The domain of leadership is shifting from circumscribed geographies to globally encompassing geographies; from a nation or domestic economy to the whole world" (Adler, 1999, p. 53). Effective global managers will do their work with an appreciation of what is different and adapt accordingly. They will learn how to leverage their own strengths and the strengths of others in response to the demands of working across distance, country borders, and cultural expectations. The effective global organization will have a plan to ensure that managers learn how to do this.

Epilogue

What's Next for the Global Manager?

It's been several years since Peter became a global manager. His developmental efforts have been successful; his colleagues in the United States and France are cognizant of his strengths and, because they see his continuing effort to improve, patient with his weaknesses. He has gained so much credibility with his direct reports in France that he is often invited to their homes for dinner when he is in the country. Some of his direct reports have recognized that if they want to move forward in their own careers, they will have to learn the same skills that Peter has learned. Peter has become a respected mentor for the generation of managers that will follow him.

Peter has moved from novice to role model. As he prepares to move to the next level of organizational responsibility, Peter knows that even more capabilities will be required. But what? On his frequent trips to France and in his daily review of the international press, Peter has, of course, become very aware of increasing social unrest that often appears to track with the spread of the global economy. He has been surprised, confused, and almost hurt that what he views as the wonders of globalization are apparently seen as threatening to many people. It is certain that Peter's multidimensionality will bring him face to face with some of these views and require him to consider issues that he has always compartmentalized as political or social—not his business!

In this book we have characterized the work of the new global manager as distinct because of its complexity and because of its difference from the commonly held view of what constitutes the work of a global manager. Looking to the future, we believe that the global manager's job will continue to become even more complicated because the role of the corporation as primarily a wealth-generating entity that answers mainly to shareholders is increasingly being called into question. This questioning is coming both from people outside corporations who fear their power and people inside organizations who believe that they have broader responsibilities. When the corporation takes multiple perspectives and serves multiple roles in society it complicates the situation further and is likely to push managers in new ways. We believe that developing political, social, and environmental awareness is an integral part of development for global managers, not something separate from it. And for Peter, this is the next step.

In this book we have directed our attention to individual managers who are striving to develop their own skills so that they can become more effective in their interactions with others—able to adapt and innovate in response to the laws, customs, and expectations of others, both virtually and from a distance. However, our primary focus has centered on managers working within the circumscribed limits of the business.

As we look ahead it becomes clear that the work of global managers is going to require participation in the debate going on in the world, both within and without corporations, regarding the present and future role of global business within the broader society.

What is the current state of the debate? What should the role of global business be at the intersection of the organization with government, nongovernmental organizations, and the social issues of a country?

Upbeat observers feel that global business will provide world-wide growth and development opportunities. According to this view, the economic impact of globalization will create employment opportunities for the world's impoverished, help create desperately needed infrastructure in developing economies, and contribute to the process of democratization and the correction of global social problems (Parker, 1996). Advocates of this view believe that business may be one of the few viable mechanisms strong enough to reverse many of the problems that currently exist.

Others, in contrast, believe that global business will lead to further and continued exploitation of foreign workers, the continued cycle of dependency between the developed and developing world, and the accelerated destruction of natural resources and local cultures. Proponents of this view argue that the forces driving global business will undermine the power of local and national governments and will weaken the ability of policymakers to control key social and economic processes. This view is illustrated by Segall, Dasen, Berry, and Poortinga (1999, p. 273): "The late twentieth-century version of a 'global economy' . . . has been an attempt to allow untrammeled 'market forces' to shape the human future. This is easily characterized as a form of neocapitalist expansion, aided and abetted by a Western cultural set of institutions . . . a movement that so far has exacerbated, rather than reduced, the gap between rich and poor everywhere."

Finally, between these two extremes are those who argue that in a compressed and interconnected world, global business and the broader society must work together to the mutual benefit of one another. Global organizations by their very existence have an impact on the social fabric of countries and therefore bear a responsibility for working with religious organizations, governments, and nongovernmental organizations to strengthen that fabric.

The Parliament of World's Religions has produced a "Global Ethic" that calls for the reduction of human abuses throughout the world. The United Nations and many national governments have written statements clarifying individual and organizational rights. And most directly related to business, nongovernmental organizations such as the World Business Council for Sustainable Development and the Caux Round Table continue to advocate for a voluntary code of corporate behavior. (Appendix B and Appendix C present two of these statements.)

The covenant of the latter organization states:

> Global business stands at the center of fundamental changes taking place in the world. These include (1) excessive poverty within countries and regions, (2) growing economic friction arising from enduring trade imbalances, which if unaddressed, can lead to political strife, (3) a gap between the increasing affluence of the developed world and the continuing poverty, concentration of population growth, and despair in less-developed countries, and (4) generational burdens, such as a polluted world and overwhelming national debts, which are passed on to children. . . . The Caux Round Table believes that business has a crucial role in helping to identify and promote solutions to issues that impede the development of a society that is more prosperous, sustainable, and equitable.

Whatever one's personal beliefs on this subject, it is increasingly evident that effective global managers must inform themselves about these issues and be prepared to at least understand the debate, if not to join in and help shape it. Global managers do not have the luxury of interacting with people from only one culture and within one country. They can no longer just attend to their knitting. Through the decisions they make in promoting the interests of their businesses, global managers affect the well-being of people in many cultures and the practices of business in many countries. As a result, global managers have a responsibility to understand what positions they are taking through their actions and must be prepared to revisit, renew, and revise those positions over time. Anyone who manages in a global context must help their organization formulate a position on its approach to wider global issues.

Mastering the skills and capacities described in this book is one step on the path to becoming an effective manager in an increasingly complicated business environment. In this book we have strongly advocated that managers need knowledge of business and culture, history and politics, customs and practices to do their work. We have discussed how managers can acquire the skills that will provide them maximum adaptability and the motivation to leverage that adaptability. But the challenges to effective management promise to become even more difficult in the future. As we consider what comes next for our readers and for our work at CCL, we see a need to help managers develop the skills to cope with the complex issues that occur at the boundaries and intersections of the organization with other social institutions.

We and several of our colleagues at CCL, in combination with a group of international research practitioners, are currently engaged in a new project that addresses one of these leadership challenges: the growing need of organizations around the world to adapt successfully to a major shift in the demographics of the workforce. This shift, caused by such factors as globalization, increased immigration, the recruitment of guest workers, and the rising influence of minority and previously disenfranchised populations across ancient ethnic, tribal, and religious divides, creates unprecedented leadership demands on organizations, their members, their practices, and their productivity.

Individuals are being asked to work side by side when their only common ground is a legacy of distrust, suspicion, and in some cases, revenge. Protestants and Catholics are recruited to work for U.S. computer companies in Northern Ireland. Bosnian and Croatian refugees work side by side in Greensboro, North Carolina, and members of each group complain to their supervisor that the other is getting preferential treatment. Indian programmers work virtually for British companies and feel resentment toward colonialist attitudes, whether real or imagined. An Asian automobile company suffers repeated work stoppages in a European production facility due to line managers' inability to create an environment in which different ethnic groups can work together. As these examples make clear, managers not only need to be able to adapt, they must also acquire the knowledge and skills to be able to lead groups of people with very different histories, perspectives, values, and cultures. In many of these cases, and on an increasing scale worldwide, managers and leaders in all types of organizations are asked to forge work teams made up of groups of people whose very identity is built on a dislike of one another.

We don't know enough yet about how to help managers prepare themselves for these enormous responsibilities. That is the work that must be continued by CCL and by other institutions working in partnership with practicing managers and leaders. Just as this book represents a collaboration between us and our research partners, we look forward to learning with you in this new venture and sharing with you what we learn.

Appendix A:
The Research Study

In this appendix we present the basics of the research that served as the catalyst for this book—the method, the measures we used, the data analysis strategy, the results, and the limitations of the work. The Center for Creative Leadership will publish a technical report describing this research from its inception for those wanting even more information (Leslie, Dalton, Ernst, & Deal, forthcoming). Four tables recording alphas and correlations can be found at the end of this appendix.

I. Method

A. Participants

Two hundred eleven managers from four organizations participated in this study. Ninety-eight of the managers were from a Swiss-based pharmaceutical company. Twenty-five worked for a U.S.-based high-tech manufacturing firm. Forty-eight worked for a Swiss-based hospitality and service organization, and forty worked for a Swedish-based truck and manufacturing construction organization. Managers within each of the four organizations were at approximately the same level.

B. Assignment to Group

Two items from a biographical measure were used to classify managers into low- and high-global-complexity groups. The first item asked, "In how many countries are you a manager?" The second item asked, "In how many time zones do you work?" In tandem, these two items form a proxy measure to assess the level of global complexity inherent in a manager's role.

The time-zone item was converted to a four-point metric to give equal weight to each item as an additive function. The item concerning number of countries was treated as a four-point scale. The two items were summed (range 2 to 8). The median for the sample was calculated (median = 3) and the total sample was divided into two groups, a low-global-complexity group with values from 2 to 3 ($n = 110$) and a high-global-complexity group with values from 4 to 8 ($n = 101$). The assignment to global complexity category was examined for each manager to ascertain that the assignment made conceptual and practical sense.

C. Characteristics of the Sample

Both low- and high-global-complexity groups predominantly consisted of well-educated males (half the sample had at least eighteen years of education) with a mean age of forty-four and forty-five, respectively. The majority of the managers in each group were educated in only one country. Members of the high-global-complexity group were more likely to have been expatriates in the past. Although forty-one countries of birth were represented in the sample, 43 percent were Northern European by birth (Germany, Sweden, and Switzerland) and 18 percent were U.S. citizens by birth. This distribution reflects the location of the corporate headquarters of the four participating organizations. Participants lived in thirty countries at the time of the study with 66.9 percent living in Switzerland, Germany, Sweden, or the United States. The high-global-complexity sample were somewhat more likely to have been in their jobs less than a year (42 percent to 28 percent).

D. Standardization of Data

We wanted to control as much extraneous variance as possible since these managers represented different functions, organizational cultures, industry types, and locations of corporate headquarters. In addition, target managers represented a particular culture (based on native country) and their raters—bosses and subordinates—also represented a variety of cultures. We investigated the influence of the culture of the target manager and the influence of organization type on the criterion measures to determine the need to standardize the data from the four organizations before merging it.

To investigate the influence of culture we created a measure to represent three cultural regions (Ronen & Shenkar, 1985): Anglo ($n = 63$), Germanic ($n = 68$), and Nordic ($n = 37$). We assigned participants to a cultural region based on their native country. This accounted for 167 of the participants. Other cultural regions that were represented in the database could not be used due to sample size. We then conducted a one-way ANOVA (Analysis of Variance) between groups to compare means of the three regions on the boss and subordinate criterion ratings.

From the boss-rater perspective, no differences were found in criterion scores as a result of the cultural region of the target manager. However, from the subordinate-rater perspective, significant differences were found on four of the five measures. Tukey's HSD test showed that the Anglo group was rated significantly higher than the Nordic group for subordinate ratings on "managing and leading," "interpersonal relationships," "knowledge and initiative," and "contextually adept."

Please note that we do not know whether these subordinate raters were of the same cultural region as the managers, only that the Anglo group had significantly higher criterion ratings from subordinates.

We repeated the above analysis to assess the impact of organizational type on boss and subordinate ratings. (Note: location of headquarters is partially confounded with organizational type as the pharmaceutical and service industry both have corporate headquarters in the same country.) Organizational type includes pharmaceutical (Switzerland), high-tech manufacturing (United States), service (Switzerland), and truck manufacturing and construction (Sweden). Although no differences were found from the boss perspective, managers in the high-tech manufacturing site (corporate headquarters in the United States) were rated significantly higher by subordinates on "interpersonal relations" than the managers in the truck and manufacturing and construction organization and the pharmaceutical organization.

In each case it was the U.S. sample receiving statistically higher ratings. Whether this can be attributed to cultural region, industry type, or location of corporate headquarters cannot be determined.

Given these results, we standardized the data within the four organizations before merging the four data sets. Standardizing the data within organizations helped control for variation due to organizational culture, business and economic context, and industry type. It did not address variation in the criterion measure attributable to the manager's functional area or the native country or cultural orientation of the target manager or the raters.

II. Measures

A. Independent Variables

1. *Personality measure.* We used the NEO PI-R to represent the personality conceptualized as the five-factor model (FFM). The NEO PI-R presents personality traits grouped into five major factors or domains (Costa & McCrae, 1992). Each domain is made up of six facets or subscales, and these six facets define each of the factor domains. The five factors and the facets that define them are listed in Exhibit A.1. This instrument was chosen because of its psychometric integrity and because of extensive research demonstrating

that these five factors do appear to be universal, if not all-inclusive, across culture (McCrae & Costa, 1997).

2. *Demographics*. Each manager filled out a participant background form indicating sex, age, native language, country of birth, and race or ethnic origin.

EXHIBIT A.1. The Five-Factor Model as Measured by the NEO PI-R.

(N) *Neuroticism:* anxiety, angry hostility, depression, self-consciousness, impulsiveness, vulnerability. Describes a general tendency to experience negative affects such as fear, sadness, embarrassment, anger, guilt, and disgust. People with high N scores tend to be less able to control their impulses and cope more poorly with stress.

(E) *Extraversion:* warmth, gregariousness, assertiveness, activity, excitement-seeking, positive emotions. Extraverts are sociable. They like people, prefer large gatherings, and are assertive, active, and talkative. They like excitement and stimulation and tend to be energetic and optimistic.

(O) *Openness:* fantasy, aesthetics, feelings, actions, ideas, values. People with high O scores have an active imagination, aesthetic sensitivity, attentiveness to inner feelings, preference for variety, intellectual curiosity, and independence of judgment. They are willing to entertain novel ideas and unconventional values and they experience emotions more keenly than closed individuals.

(A) *Agreeableness:* trust, straightforwardness, altruism, compliance, modesty, tender-mindedness. This is a domain of interpersonal tendencies. The agreeable person is altruistic, sympathetic to others, and eager to help them, trusting and cooperative rather than competitive.

(C) *Conscientiousness:* competence, order, dutifulness, achievement striving, self-discipline, deliberation. The person with a high C score is purposeful, strong-willed and determined, achievement oriented, scrupulous, punctual, and reliable.

3. *Experiences*. Each manager filled out a participant background form indicating tenure, years in current role, expatriate experience, languages spoken in the course of doing work, languages spoken before age thirteen, number of countries lived in, country currently living in, years of formal education, number of countries educated in, and major field of study. Managers were also asked to indicate for their most recent domestic job the relationship, sex, race or ethnic origin, age, native country, country of current residence, and functional area for ten members of their work group.

4. *Roles*. Guided by the theoretical work of Mintzberg (1973) and Kaplan (1997), a seven-scale measure of fifty-six items was developed to represent role behavior. The scales were labeled Monitor, Spokesperson, Leader, Liaison, Decision Making, Negotiator, and Innovator. They represented the major categories of manager behavior defined by Mintzberg (1990, 1994) as Managing Information, Managing People, and Managing Action.

5. *Capabilities*
   a. Learning scales. Fifteen items were used to represent the learning constructs *cultural adaptability, self-development,* and *perspective-taking*. These items were derived from existing instruments (SKILLSCOPE: Kaplan, 1997; Prospector: McCall, Spreitzer, & Mahoney, 1996) and the literature.
   b. Knowledge. Eight items were used to represent the *business knowledge* construct. Nine items were used to represent the *international business knowledge* construct. Four items were used to represent the *insightful* construct. These items were derived from an existing instrument (Prospector: McCall, Spreitzer, & Mahoney, 1996) and the literature.
   c. Resilience. Four items were used to represent the resilience construct of *coping*. Seven items were used to represent *time management* and three items were used to represent *integrity*. These items were derived from an existing instrument (SKILLSCOPE: Kaplan, 1997) and the literature.

Scales and items that were significantly related to the criterion measures have been presented as part of Exercises 4.2 and 4.3 in Chapter Four. Only scales that were significantly related to either boss or subordinate performance ratings in the high- or low-global-complexity condition are represented in the tables at the end of this appendix.

B. Dependent Variables

To represent managerial performance, twenty-seven items were pulled from the literature and supplemented and revised in consultation with the first sponsor company. Conceptually, the twenty-seven items were written to address three dimensions of managerial performance: business practices and outcomes, managerial and leadership qualities, and relationships. However, results from a series of analyses and discussions suggested that the items were better represented as five factors rather than three. The first scale is called *Management and Leadership*. It represents the traditional leadership behaviors of setting direction, inspiring, and motivating. It also includes items referencing an internal focus and traditional manager-subordinate activities such as selection, development, coaching, and managing conflict. The second scale is called *Interpersonal Relationships*. This scale represents relationships internal to the organization with peers and senior managers. The third scale is called *Knowledge and Initiative*. These items combine the characteristics of broad knowledge and professional competence with the personal attributes of confidence, independence, and initiative. The fourth scale is called *Success Orientation*. This scale represents an orientation toward goal achievement and attainment of desired organizational outcomes. It also includes an item on potential to reach the most senior job in the company. The fifth scale is called *Contextually Adept*. This scale is related to the ability to manage external relationships. Scales and items have been presented in Exhibit 1.1 (What Do We Mean by Effectiveness?) in Chapter One. (The fifth scale, Contextually Adept, is not reflected in the results section, as there were no statistically significant relationships to report.)

It is interesting that these five criterion measures link conceptually to Laurent's work (1986) on cultural manifestations of effective managerial performance: technical creativity (German and Swiss), ambition and drive (American), skills in interpersonal relations and communication (Dutch and British), and the ability to manage power relationships effectively (French).

III. Data Analysis and Results

Managers participating in the study were asked to complete the 240-item personality measure, NEO PI-R; the biographical form, and the measure of role skills and capabilities. The surveys were all in English. Managers were assured that their individual results would be available only to the research team.

On the personality measure managers rated themselves on a five-point scale ranging from "strongly disagree" to "strongly agree."

On the measure of role skills and capabilities managers were asked to first rate each item on a three-point scale ranging from "this is not important to my current job" to "this is extremely important to my current job." They were then asked to go back through the items and rate their own skill at performing each of the behaviors on a five-point scale ranging from "this skill or perspective is something I am not able to do" to "this skill or perspective is one of my greatest strengths."

The boss and up to five of the manager's direct reports were asked to respond to the twenty-seven-item performance statements on a five-point scale ranging from "Strongly disagree" to "Strongly agree." A "not applicable" response category was provided. This measure was in English. These responses were returned directly to the Center. Respondents were assured that their individual responses would remain confidential to the research team.

Participating organizations were also assured that the results from their company would be confidential. A proprietary report describing in-company results was prepared for each of the sponsor companies.

The data analysis and results are organized by the questions of interest.

Question 1: What do global managers do?

Managers in high-global-complexity jobs were statistically more likely to endorse the role behaviors of spokesperson ($t = -.284, p < .01$) and liaison ($t = -2.35, p < .05$) as extremely important to their current job and the capabilities of cultural adaptability ($t = -8.27$, $p < .0001$), international business knowledge ($t = -7.69, p < .001$), and time management ($t = -2.05, p < .05$). Managers in low-global-complexity jobs were statistically more likely to endorse only the role behavior of leader as extremely important to their current job ($t = 1.91, p < .05$). The two groups did not differ in the importance they ascribed to the roles of monitor, decision maker, negotiator, or innovator and they did not differ in the importance they ascribed to the remaining capabilities: self-development, perspective-taking, business knowledge, insight, coping, and integrity.

Discussion. Managers working domestically identified the role of leader as being significantly more important to their effectiveness, whereas global managers attributed significantly more importance to the roles of liaison, spokesperson, and negotiator. This finding suggests that as work responsibility becomes more globally complex, managers place less emphasis on the internal role of leader-subordinate relationships and place greater emphasis on external roles that take place at the organization's periphery. Global managers also attributed significantly more importance to the skill of time management, international business knowledge, and cultural adaptability than did their domestic counterparts. These results track with our definition of global manager: one who manages and leads across distance, country borders, and cultural expectations.

Question 2: What does it take for the manager to be effective when the work is global in scope, and is it different from what it takes to be effective when the work is domestic in scope?

Zero order correlations were conducted between the independent and dependent variables for the two rater groups within the low- and high-global-complexity condition. The correlations for boss and subordinate criterion measures for the high- and low-global-complexity groups are provided in Tables A.1 to A.4 at the end of this appendix. Because there were no significant relationships for the criterion measure Contextually Adept, it has been dropped from the tables. There were also no significant findings for the independent variables of Time Management, Integrity, Self-Development, and Insightful, so these results have also been dropped from the tables for greater ease of presentation.

Discussion. A. *Personality.* An examination of the results for the high- and low-global-complexity managers as reviewed from the boss rating perspective reveals that Neuroticism was related to criterion ratings for managers in jobs with both high and low global complexity. Conscientiousness was related to criterion ratings for managers only in the high-global-complexity condition. Conversely, Extraversion was significantly related to boss criterion measures only in the low-global-complexity condition. In the low-global-complexity condition the management and leadership criterion scale was a better criterion measure. In the high-global-complexity condition the Knowledge and Initiative criterion measure was more salient.

These results track with the interpretation of the importance data regarding what managers in high- and low-global-complexity jobs do. Managers in low-global-complexity jobs are more focused internally on manager-leader relationships, hence Neuroticism and Extraversion are differentiators on this criterion measure. Managers in high-global-complexity jobs are more focused externally, hence

Neuroticism and Conscientiousness in support of doing the work are better differentiators.

The subordinate results present a different picture. In the low-global-complexity condition Conscientiousness is related to all four criterion measures. The high-global-complexity results for subordinates track the results obtained with the boss data in the high-global-complexity condition for the Conscientiousness criterion relationship. The Neuroticism variable is significantly and negatively correlated with Interpersonal Relationships in the low- but not the high-global-complexity condition.

B. *Roles*. For boss criterion ratings in the high-global-complexity condition, skill in playing the roles of leader, decision maker, negotiator, and innovator were significantly related to three of the four criterion measures. The relationship of the Negotiator to the criterion management and leadership can probably be attributed to two items in that scale that speak to managing and leading from a distance. Otherwise the manager-leader criterion seems more salient in the low-global-complexity condition than in the high-global-complexity condition, as was the case with the personality results. Decision Maker works similarly in both low- and high-global-complexity conditions. Negotiator and Innovator are significantly related to performance only in the high-global-complexity condition. It is interesting but inexplicable that skill in playing the role of spokesperson and liaison are only statistically significant for the low-global-complexity condition even though both of these roles were endorsed by managers in the high-global-complexity condition as more important to their jobs. Leader is related to the criterion Knowledge and Initiative in the high-global-complexity condition.

For the subordinate data in the low-global-complexity condition, the relationship of both Leader and Decision Maker scales to the criterion track the results of the boss data in the low-global-complexity condition. In the high-global-complexity condition, only skill playing the role of Decision Maker is statistically significant and follows the pattern for the high-global-complexity condition of the boss data.

C. *Capabilities*

1. Learning scales. For the learning scales, cultural adaptability and perspective-taking are significantly related to criterion measures only in the high-global-complexity condition and only for the boss data. These two scales were unrelated to subordinate ratings in the high-global-complexity condition, and an interesting poverty of significant results is beginning to emerge from the high-global-complexity subordinate ratings condition. Contrary to our hypotheses, in the low-global-complexity condition subordinates give higher criterion scores on Knowledge and Initiative and Success Orientation to managers who have the capability of cultural adaptability. This result can be attributed to a confound with expatriate experience.

2. Knowledge scales. For the knowledge scales from the boss perspective, core business knowledge and international business knowledge are significantly related to the criterion in the high- but not the low-global-complexity condition. From the subordinate perspective, there are no significant relationships in the high-global-complexity condition. In the low-global-complexity condition core business knowledge and international business knowledge are significantly related to subordinate ratings of both Knowledge and Initiative and Success Orientation.

3. Resilience. The Coping scale is related to boss criterion ratings in both the low- and high-global-complexity condition. It is not related to subordinate ratings in either condition. Time Management, although identified by managers in the high-global-complexity condition as most important to their job, is not significantly related to any of the performance criteria.

4. Experience. Again, for the sake of parsimony, only those variables that appear to be of conceptual interest are reported in Tables A.1 to A.4—the number of countries one has lived in, whether or not one has been an expatriate, and the number of languages one speaks. Only expatriate experience was significantly related to sub-

ordinate ratings of Interpersonal Relationships, and it was in the low-global-complexity condition. Further investigation revealed that when expatriate experience was held constant, the significance of international business knowledge and cultural adaptability to subordinate criterion ratings in the low-global-complexity condition disappeared. For whatever reason, subordinates in this low-global-complexity condition valued expatriate experience in managers. These experience variables were not significantly related to boss ratings of performance in either condition.

In summary, we conclude that the subordinate ratings in the high-global-complexity condition offer little to enhance our understanding except for the power of the Conscientiousness and Decision Making constructs to obtain significance in spite of the noise in the data that we attribute to having multiple raters in multiple locations. We would normally simply abandon these results, but in this case we think that the failure of most variables to obtain significance under the high-global-complexity condition for subordinate ratings reflects the reality of the work of global managers—their direct reports are scattered around the world. Each evaluates global managers through a different lens, and the average of these scores is mush! The manager must be able to adapt to each subordinate as appropriate to distance and culture.

The boss ratings are potentially more interesting. Skill in playing the role of Decision Maker and Leader might be construed as "same but different." They were related to high performance ratings in the high- and low-global-complexity condition. However, one might safely surmise, given the work of people such as Dorfman (1996), Adler (1997), and Smith and Schwartz (forthcoming), that even though these skills are the same vis-à-vis the relationship to performance criteria for both groups, they must be enacted differently based on culture.

Here we would suggest that perhaps it is skill in playing the role of innovator, as well as the capabilities of cultural adaptability, perspective-taking, and international business knowledge unique to the high-global-complexity (boss ratings) condition that allow the effective global manager to make the necessary adaptation—to adapt what is the "same" as appropriate to the complex context of distance, country, and culture.

Question 3. How do managers develop the capabilities of the effective global manager?

This is a conceptual section. It is built on the significant albeit modest statistical relationships that exist between the boss criterion measures and what we will now call the pivotal skills: cultural adaptability, international business knowledge, perspective-taking, and ability to play the role of innovator in a high-global-complexity condition. In this section we will replace our initial framework for understanding with an integrated framework for development.

There is a significant relationship between the five personality variables and the four pivotal capabilities. Cultural adaptability and international business knowledge are related negatively to Neuroticism and positively to Conscientiousness. This could be interpreted to mean that individuals able to tolerate the ambiguity and the relativity of what they "know" (low Neuroticism) and who possess the determination and persistence to learn new ways of doing things (high Conscientiousness) will be more likely to acquire the knowledge and skill to do business in culturally appropriate ways in other cultures. Individuals who have some appreciation for their own personality will have a greater appreciation for how hard or easy it might be for them to acquire the skills associated with cultural adaptability and international business knowledge.

Looking at the experience variables—languages spoken, countries lived in, and past expatriate experience—the person who has the skills of cultural adaptability and international business knowledge is also likely to speak more languages, have lived in more places, and have been an expatriate. These skill sets are related to particular experiences that are related to performance. It is interesting that experience and personality are not significantly related to one another. Individuals who learn where these skills can be acquired may be encouraged to learn languages, travel, and seek out expatriate experience with focused understanding of what it is they are trying to learn as part of the experience.

Individuals who are skilled at perspective-taking—seeing the world through someone else's eyes—are more likely to have high scores on the trait of Agreeableness. In other words, these managers are more or less hard-wired toward empathy. One might surmise that those with low Agreeableness scores might have a harder time learning the skill of perspective-taking. Even though Agreeableness is not directly related to performance, it is related to skills associated with taking the perspective of others.

Finally, individuals who are skilled playing the role of innovator—creating a new way of working out of two seemingly opposing ways—also have high scores on the traits of Openness to Experience and Extraversion. These managers are inclined to see novel associations and are also able to sell or persuade others to see these new possibilities. It is interesting that the ability to play the role of innovator is also statistically related to the number of languages a person speaks. So managers aspiring to global responsibility might be strongly encouraged to learn another language—even if they never become skilled enough to use this language in the course of doing business. Taking on the grammar and syntax of another language must surely be a way to prime one's brain to look for novel associations in other countries. The relationship of Openness to ability to play the role of innovator rather than evidencing a direct relationship with the performance criteria in the high-global-complexity condition is particularly interesting. Although C (Conscientiousness) and N (Neuroticism) along with cognitive ability have become generally accepted predictors of performance across a wide range of jobs, O (Openness) has been limited to predictions of training proficiency (see Exhibit A.1). A recent article by LePine, Colquitt, and Erez (2000) points to the predictive power of O beyond cognitive ability and C in situations requiring adaptability. LePine et al. define adaptability as requiring unlearning and re-learning. In the case of high global complexity, O is playing as an antecedent to the ability to behave innovatively and creatively and innovativeness is being conceptualized as one of the pivotal skills that allows managers to adapt what they know how to do to the situation at hand as the context shifts.

Certain skills and capabilities are common to managerial work whether that work be global or domestic. This is what Mintzberg said many years ago. However, subsequent work on culture tells us that how these common roles are played out must differ as the cultural context, country infrastructure, and distance shift and interact. Someone able to make that shift will have very specialized knowledge and unique personal capabilities. We propose that a person wishing to develop this specialized knowledge and these unique personal capabilities will benefit from an understanding of who he or she is (personality) and from knowing the kinds of experiences that facilitate the development of this knowledge and those capabilities: traveling, learning other languages, and having focused expatriate experience, to name three.

IV. Limitations

This work is limited in the following ways and so must be considered as an early step in understanding management and leadership in complex contexts. Although the sample size is international, most cultural regions of the world, with the exception of the Anglo, Germanic, and Nordic regions, are severely underrepresented. The sample sizes are small, so it is not possible to do the kind of structural equation modeling that would confirm or fail to confirm the proposed integrated framework for development. We did not obtain data on the native country of the boss and subordinates for the entire sample and therefore cannot do a comprehensive analysis of the impact of cultural similarity on criterion ratings. We do not know whether the boss, subordinates, and target managers are co-located. We do not account for the functional specialty of the manager. These data are also influenced by rater bias. Managers rated themselves on all the personality and the role and capability scales. Also, the shared variance among the independent variables interferes with the ability to use regression methodology, since the first variable into the equation accounts for the significant relationships—regardless of theory or what is entered first. Finally, the instrumentation was designed in the West by Americans, and the surveys were administered in English. The criterion measures were focused primarily on activities that occur inside the organization and not on activities that occur outside or at the boundaries. In other words, there is a lot of noise and error in these data, and this seems to be particularly apparent in the criterion ratings from subordinates in the low-global-complexity condition.

Nonetheless, this work makes a unique contribution to the understanding of the work of the manager in this age of globalization. The work is quantitative in an arena replete with best practices, interview data, and case studies of exceptional individuals. The work considers and integrates a broad number of variables that emerge from various theoretical perspectives that have been found to have different kinds of relationships to managerial effectiveness criteria. The subject pool is international and the organizations they work for represent a variety of industry types in a variety of locations.

We look forward to further developments in this area and invite our colleagues to use our measurement tools to replicate and expand our work.

TABLE A.1. Alphas and Intercorrelations Among Personality, International Experience, Role Behaviors, Capabilities, and Performance Variables—Boss Ratings, Low Global Complexity.

Variable	1	2	3	4	5	6	7	8	9	10	11	12	13	14	15	16	17	18	19	20	21	22	23	24
1 Neuroticism	.80	-.40	-.13	-.10	-.27	-.13	-.34	-.19	-.22	-.11	-.07	-.23	-.07	-.11	-.09	-.09	.00	.01	.10	-.10	-.22	-.12	-.17	-.23
2 Extraversion		.74	.42	.03	.18	.16	.23	.08	.30	.27	.21	.30	.13	.30	.13	.09	.03	-.02	-.01	.08	.20	.01	.06	.11
3 Openness			.74	.34	-.04	.01	.03	.02	-.01	.08	.04	.06	.05	.25	.01	.05	.07	.08	.03	.11	-.06	-.11	.04	-.05
4 Agreeableness				.73	.06	-.14	.01	.01	-.24	.08	-.02	-.06	-.06	-.07	-.19	-.03	.20	-.17	.23	-.17	-.10	.01	-.11	-.12
5 Conscientiousness					.81	.29	.18	.25	.14	.26	.15	.28	.29	.04	.20	.17	.15	-.11	-.17	.11	.08	.03	.15	.17
6 Core business knowledge						.78	.54	.49	.52	.46	.51	.50	.68	.43	.55	.51	.44	-.01	-.18	.14	.08	.03	.14	.17
7 Coping							.68	.51	.51	.61	.46	.65	.49	.56	.30	.24	.52	-.11	-.01	.05	.14	.02	.12	.22
8 Monitor								.68	.34	.47	.31	.56	.43	.43	.20	.19	.43	-.10	.11	-.04	.15	.01	.19	.18
9 Spokesperson									.80	.44	.56	.51	.43	.45	.52	.31	.40	.03	-.05	.03	.33	.19	.25	.26
10 Leader										.90	.45	.65	.53	.49	.23	.36	.61	-.05	.09	-.02	.23	.14	.18	.20
11 Liaison											.75	.43	.48	.41	.40	.42	.32	-.10	.05	.00	.13	.16	.15	.21
12 Decision maker												.87	.58	.54	.26	.22	.41	.05	-.10	.00	.21	.02	.21	.21
13 Negotiator													.79	.46	.53	.48	.42	-.10	.03	-.06	.05	.02	.13	.07

	14	15	16	17	18	19	20	21	22	23	24
14 Ability to play the role of innovator	.83	.32	.33	.33	.10	-.15	.15	.01	-.04	.16	.05
15 International business knowledge		.91	.67	.25	-.01	.03	.09	.12	.18	.15	.13
16 Cultural adaptability			.85	.34	.02	-.27	.35	-.02	.09	.04	.08
17 Perspective–taking				.70	.05	-.02	.11	.09	.09	.09	.10
18 Number languages					xx	-.09	.23	.07	-.04	.10	.09
19 Expatriate						xx	-.68	.06	.08	.06	.04
20 Number countries							xx	-.02	-.04	-.02	-.03
21 Managing–leading								.87	.67	.65	.77
22 Interpersonal relationships									.80	.45	.67
23 Knowledge–initiative										.78	.69
24 Success orientation											.68

TABLE A.2. Alphas and Intercorrelations Among Personality, International Experience, Role Behaviors, Capabilities, and Performance Variables—Boss Ratings, High Global Complexity.

Variable	1	2	3	4	5	6	7	8	9	10	11	12	13	14	15	16	17	18	19	20	21	22	23	24
1 Neuroticism	.80	-.16	.05	-.33	-.43	-.44	-.50	-.41	-.22	-.27	-.28	-.41	-.37	-.17	-.23	-.22	-.11	.00	.08	-.07	-.01	.00	-.23	-.07
2 Extraversion		.74	.45	.23	.20	.19	.22	.25	.42	.23	.37	.25	.13	.27	.07	.02	.11	.10	.13	-.08	-.03	.00	.09	.04
3 Openness			.74	.14	-.17	-.04	.15	.09	.21	.05	.16	.05	.00	.25	-.05	-.11	.18	.02	.06	-.04	-.04	-.02	-.02	-.01
4 Agreeableness				.73	.27	-.01	.16	.03	.19	.28	.17	.11	.17	-.01	.00	.15	.32	.00	.05	.00	.10	.18	.02	.00
5 Conscientiousness					.81	.36	.17	.24	.25	.25	.21	.36	.42	.12	.34	.28	.10	.05	-.05	.08	.12	.00	.34	.30
6 Core business knowledge						.78	.16	.49	.35	.57	.52	.68	.65	.43	.61	.51	.17	.23	-.23	.25	-.04	-.10	.32	.19
7 Coping							.68	.42	.42	.60	.55	.57	.50	.50	.45	.43	.43	.16	-.08	.12	.08	.05	.36	.26
8 Monitor								.68	.50	.43	.40	.52	.42	.44	.29	.26	.25	.07	.13	.00	.11	.00	.14	.15
9 Spokesperson									.80	.56	.52	.40	.44	.55	.43	.46	.34	.30	.09	.01	.12	-.03	.19	.01
10 Leader										.90	.54	.66	.68	.49	.52	.71	.59	.27	.01	.11	.18	-.03	.27	.06
11 Liaison											.75	.54	.47	.51	.43	.51	.45	.29	.03	.18	-.03	.07	.17	.13
12 Decision maker												.87	.66	.48	.25	.23	.29	.25	-.20	.24	.17	.00	.38	.25
13 Negotiator													.79	.42	.69	.66	.50	.26	-.14	.13	.22	.16	.38	.26

14 Ability to play role of innovator	.83	.38	.34	.29	.21	.02	.06	.09	.02	.24	.10
15 International business knowledge	.91	.51	.40	.44	-.28	.45	.13	.00	.39	.22	
16 Cultural adaptability	.85	.43	.40	-.21	.45	.15	-.08	.26	.14		
17 Perspective–taking	.70	.17	.07	.07	.17	.23	.21	.17			
18 Number languages	xx	-.28	.29	.10	-.20	.14	-.06				
19 Expatriate	xx	-.64	-.02	-.03	-.13	-.06					
20 Number countries	xx	-.08	-.09	.00	.08						
21 Managing–leading	.87	.70	.63	.63							
22 Interpersonal relationships	.80	.33	.51								
23 Knowledge–initiative	.78	.64									
24 Success orientation	.68										

TABLE A.3. Alphas and Intercorrelations Among Personality, International Experience, Role Behaviors, Capabilities, and Performance Variables—Subordinate Ratings, Low Global Complexity.

Variable	1	2	3	4	5	6	7	8	9	10	11	12	13	14	15	16	17	18	19	20	21	22	23	24
1 Neuroticism	.80	-.40	-.13	-.10	-.27	-.13	-.34	-.19	-.22	-.11	-.07	-.23	-.07	-.11	-.09	-.09	.00	.00	.10	-.10	.02	-.22	.05	.01
2 Extraversion		.74	.42	.03	.18	.16	.23	.08	.30	.27	.21	.30	.13	.30	.13	.09	.03	-.01	.08	.20	.02	.10	-.01	.01
3 Openness			.74	.34	-.04	.01	.03	.02	-.01	.08	.04	.06	.05	.25	.01	.05	.07	.08	.03	.11	.08	.02	.09	.04
4 Agreeableness				.73	.06	-.14	.01	.01	-.24	.08	-.02	-.06	-.06	-.07	-.19	-.03	.20	-.17	.23	-.17	.07	.08	-.01	-.04
5 Conscientiousness					.81	.29	.18	.25	.14	.26	.15	.28	.29	.04	.20	.17	.15	-.11	-.17	.11	.29	.22	.27	.29
6 Core business knowledge						.78	.54	.49	.52	.46	.51	.50	.68	.43	.55	.51	.44	-.01	-.18	.14	.10	.15	.26	.20
7 Coping							.68	.51	.51	.61	.46	.65	.49	.56	.30	.24	.52	-.11	-.01	.05	.07	.16	.18	.19
8 Monitor								.68	.34	.47	.31	.56	.43	.43	.20	.19	.43	-.10	.11	-.04	.09	.00	.19	.10
9 Spokesperson									.80	.44	.56	.51	.43	.45	.52	.31	.40	.03	-.05	.03	.12	.16	.17	.15
10 Leader										.90	.45	.65	.53	.49	.23	.36	.61	-.05	.09	-.02	.20	.03	.18	.16
11 Liaison											.75	.43	.48	.41	.40	.42	.32	-.11	.05	.00	.10	.11	.18	.14
12 Decision maker												.87	.58	.54	.26	.22	.41	.05	-.10	.00	.14	.07	.25	.20
13 Negotiator													.79	.46	.53	.48	.42	-.10	.03	-.06	.10	.09	.20	.21

	14	15	16	17	18	19	20	21	22	23	24
14 Ability to play the role of innovator	.83	.32	.33	.10	-.15	.15	-.02	-.05	.16	.07	
15 International business knowledge		.91	.67	.25	.03	.09	.10	.15	.22	.22	
16 Cultural adaptability			.85	.34	.02	-.27	.35	.14	.15	.21	.25
17 Perspective–taking				.70	.05	-.02	.11	.07	.01	.09	.02
18 Number languages					xx	.04	.05	.04	.03	-.01	-.03
19 Expatriate						xx	-.68	-.13	-.18	-.06	-.13
20 Number countries							xx	.10	.20	.08	.08
21 Managing–leading								.87	.67	.65	.77
22 Interpersonal relations									.80	.45	.67
23 Knowledge–initiative										.78	.69
24 Success orientation											.68

TABLE A.4. Alphas and Intercorrelations Among Personality, International Experience, Role Behaviors, Capabilities, and Performance Variables—Subordinate Ratings, High Global Complexity.

Variable	1	2	3	4	5	6	7	8	9	10	11	12	13	14	15	16	17	18	19	20	21	22	23	24
1 Neuroticism	.80	-.16	.05	-.33	-.43	-0.4	-.50	-.41	-.22	-.27	-.28	-.41	-.37	-.17	-.23	-.22	-.11	.00	.08	-.07	.02	-.06	-.10	-.07
2 Extraversion		.74	.45	.23	.20	.19	.22	.25	.42	.23	.37	.25	.13	.27	.07	.02	.11	.10	.13	-.08	.03	.12	.10	.09
3 Openness			.74	.14	-.17	-.04	.15	.09	.21	.05	.16	.05	.00	.25	-.05	-.11	.18	.02	.06	-.04	.10	.09	.06	.00
4 Agreeableness				.73	.27	-.01	.16	.03	.19	.28	.17	.11	.17	-.01	.00	.15	.32	.00	.05	.00	-.02	.12	-.02	-.10
5 Conscientiousness					.81	.36	.17	.24	.25	.25	.21	.36	.42	.12	.34	.28	.10	.05	-.05	.08	.00	.06	.20	.20
6 Core business knowledge						.78	.62	.49	.35	.57	.52	.68	.65	.43	.61	.62	.40	.44	-.23	.25	-.07	-.11	.09	.08
7 Coping							.68	.42	.42	.60	.55	.57	.50	.50	.45	.43	.43	.16	-.08	.12	.10	.08	.15	.13
8 Monitor								.68	.50	.43	.40	.52	.42	.44	.29	.26	.25	.07	.13	.00	.10	.04	.15	.18
9 Spokesperson									.80	.56	.52	.40	.44	.55	.43	.46	.34	.30	.09	.01	.12	.12	.08	.08
10 Leader										.90	.54	.66	.68	.49	.52	.71	.59	.27	.01	.11	.09	.03	.03	.05
11 Liaison											.75	.47	.52	.51	.53	.51	.45	.29	.03	.18	-.03	-.02	-.01	-.06
12 Decision maker												.87	.61	.48	.25	.23	.29	.25	-.20	.24	.07	-.01	.21	.21
13 Negotiator													.79	.42	.69	.66	.50	.26	-.14	.13	.00	-.02	-.01	.04

14 Ability to play role of innovator	.83	.38	.34	.29	.21	.02	.06	.06	-.02	.17	.16
15 International business knowledge		.91	.74	.41	.44	-.42	.45	-.03	-.03	.08	.10
16 Cultural adaptability			.85	.53	.40	-.21	.45	.03	-.03	.04	.02
17 Perspective-taking				.70	.17	.07	.07	.00	.04	-.07	-.17
18 Number languages					xx	-.28	.29	-.05	-.09	-.04	-.08
19 Expatriate						xx	-.64	.06	-.03	-.02	.06
20 Number countries							xx	.09	.09	.14	.17
21 Managing-leading								.87	.83	.75	.74
22 Interpersonal relationships									.80	.67	.67
23 Knowledge-initiative										.78	.80
24 Success orientation											.6

Appendix B:
An International Code
of Business Ethics

Section 1. Preamble

The mobility of employment, capital, products, and technology is making business increasingly global in its transactions and its effects.

Laws and market forces are necessary but insufficient guides for conduct.

Responsibility for the policies and actions of business and respect for the dignity and interests of its stakeholders are fundamental.

Shared values, including a commitment to shared prosperity, are as important for a global community as for communities of smaller scale.

For these reasons, and because business can be a powerful agent of positive social change, we offer the following principles as a foundation for dialogue and action by business leaders in search of business responsibility. In so doing, we affirm the necessity for moral values in business decision-making. With them, stable business relationships and a sustainable world community are impossible.

Developed in 1994 by the Caux Round Table in Switzerland and printed in *Business Ethics: The Magazine of Socially Responsible Business*, 10(1), January-February 1996. Used by permission of the Caux Round Table.

Section 2: General Principles

Principle 1: The Responsibilities of Business: Beyond Shareholders Toward Stakeholders

The value of a business to society is the wealth and employment it creates and the marketable products and services it provides to consumers at a reasonable price commensurate with quality. To create such value, a business must maintain its own economic health and viability, but survival is not a sufficient goal.

Businesses have a role to play in improving the lives of all their customers, employees, and shareholders by sharing with them the wealth they have created. Suppliers and competitors as well should expect businesses to honor their obligations in a spirit of honesty and fairness. As responsible citizens of the local, national, regional, and global communities in which they operate, businesses share a part in shaping the future of those economies.

Principle 2: The Economic and Social Impact of Business: Toward Innovation, Justice and World Community

Businesses established in foreign countries to develop, produce, or sell should also contribute to the social advancement of those countries by creating productive employment and helping to raise the purchasing power of their citizens. Businesses also should contribute to human rights, education, welfare, and the vitalization of the countries in which they operate.

Businesses should contribute to economic and social development not only in the countries in which they operate, but also in the world community at large, through the effective and prudent use of resources, free and fair competition, and emphasis upon innovation in technology, production methods, marketing and communications.

Principle 3: Business Behavior: Beyond the Letter of the Law Toward a Spirit of Trust

While accepting the legitimacy of trade secrets, businesses should recognize that sincerity, candor, truthfulness, the keeping of promises and transparency contribute not only to their own credibility and stability but also to the smoothness and efficiency of business transactions, particularly on the international level.

Principle 4: Respect for Rules

To avoid trade frictions and to promote freer trade, equal conditions for competition, and fair, equitable treatment for all participants, businesses should respect international and domestic rules. In addition, they should recognize that some behavior, although legal, may still have adverse consequences.

Principle 5: Support for Multilateral Trade

Businesses should support the multilateral trade systems of the GATT/World Trade Organization and similar international agreements. They should cooperate in efforts to promote the progressive and judicious liberalization of trade, and to relax those domestic measures that unreasonably hinder global commerce, while giving due respect to national policy objectives.

Principle 6: Respect for the Environment

A business should protect and, where possible, improve the environment, promote sustainable development, and prevent the wasteful use of natural resources.

Principle 7: Avoidance of Illicit Operations

A business should not participate in or condone bribery, money laundering, or other corrupt practices: indeed, it should seek cooperation with others to eliminate them. It should not trade in arms, or other materials used for terrorist activities, drug traffic, or other organized crime.

Section 3: Stakeholder Principles

Customers

We believe in treating all customers with dignity, irrespective of whether they purchase our products and services directly from us or otherwise acquire them in the market. We therefore have a responsibility to:

> Provide our customers with the highest quality products and services consistent with their requirements;
>
> Treat our customers fairly in all aspects of our business transactions, including a high level of service and remedies for their dissatisfaction;
>
> Make every effort to ensure that the health and safety of our customers, as well as the quality of their environment, will be sustained or enhanced by our products and services;
>
> Assure respect for human dignity in products offered, marketing, and advertising; and
>
> Respect the integrity of the culture of our customers.

Employees

We believe in the dignity of every employee and in taking employee interest seriously. We therefore have the responsibility to:

> Provide jobs and compensation that improve workers' living conditions;
>
> Provide working conditions that respect each employee's health and dignity;

Be honest in communications with employees and open in sharing information, limited only by legal and competitive restraints;

Listen to, and where possible, act on employees' suggestions, ideas, requests, and complaints;

Engage in good faith negotiations when conflict arises;

Avoid discriminatory practices and guarantee equal treatment and opportunity in areas such as gender, age, race, and religion;

Promote in the business itself the employment of differently abled people in places of work where they can be genuinely useful;

Protect employees from avoidable injury and illness in the workplace;

Encourage and assist employees in developing relevant and transferable skills and knowledge; and

Be sensitive to serious unemployment problems frequently associated with business decisions and work with governments, employee groups, other agencies and each other in addressing these dislocations.

Owners-Investors

We believe in honoring the trust our investors place in us. We therefore have a responsibility to:

Apply professional and diligent management in order to secure a fair and competitive return on our owners' investment;

Disclose relevant information to owners-investors subject only to legal requirements and competitive constraints;

Conserve, protect, and increase the owners-investors' assets; and

Respect owners-investors' requests, suggestions, complaints and formal resolutions.

Suppliers

Our relationship with suppliers and subcontractors must be based on mutual respect. We therefore have a responsibility to:

Seek fairness and truthfulness in all of our activities, including pricing, licensing, and rights to sell;

Ensure that our business activities are free from coercion and unnecessary litigation;

Foster long-term stability in the supplier relationship in return for value, quality, competitiveness, and reliability;

Share information with suppliers and integrate them into our planning process;

Pay suppliers on time and in accordance with agreed terms of trade;

Seek, encourage, and prefer suppliers and subcontractors whose employment practices respect human dignity.

Competitors

We believe that fair economic competition is one of the basic requirements for increasing the wealth of nations and, ultimately, for making possible the just distribution of goods and services. We therefore have a responsibility to:

Promote competitive behavior that is socially and environmentally beneficial and demonstrates mutual respect among competitors;

Refrain from either seeking or participating in questionable payments or favors to secure competitive advantages;

Respect both tangible and intellectual property rights; and

Refuse to acquire commercial information by dishonest or unethical means, such as industrial espionage.

Communities

We believe that as global corporate citizens, we can contribute to such forces of reform and human rights as are at work in the communities in which they operate. We therefore have a responsibility in these communities to:

Respect human rights and democratic institutions, and promote them wherever practicable;

Recognize government's legitimate obligation to society at large and support public policies and practices that promote human development through harmonious relations between business and other segments of society;

Collaborate with those forces in the community dedicated to raising standards of health, education, workplace safety, and economic well-being;

Promote and stimulate sustainable development and play a leading role in preserving and enhancing the physical environment and conserving the earth's resources;

Support peace, security, diversity, and social integration;

Respect the integrity of local cultures; and

Be a good corporate citizen through charitable donations, educational and cultural contributions, and employee participation in community and civic affairs.

Appendix C:
U.N. Code of Human Rights

Article 1

All human beings are born free and equal in dignity and rights. They are endowed with reason and conscience and should act towards one another in a spirit of brotherhood.

Article 2

Everyone is entitled to all the rights and freedoms set forth in this Declaration, without distinction of any kind, such as race, colour, sex, religion, political or other opinion, national or social origin, property, birth, or other status.

Article 3

Everyone has the right to life, liberty, and security of person.

Article 4

No one shall be held in slavery or servitude; slavery and the slave trade shall be prohibited in all forms.

Article 5

No one shall be subjected to torture or to cruel, inhuman, or degrading treatment or punishment.

Used by permission of United Nations Publications.

Article 6

Everyone has the right to recognition everywhere as a person before the law.

Article 7

All are equal before the law and are entitled without any discrimination to equal protection of the law. All are entitled to equal protection against any discrimination in violation of this Declaration and against any incitement to such discrimination.

Article 8

Everyone has the right to an effective remedy by the competent national tribunals for acts violating the fundamental rights granted him by the constitution or by law.

Article 9

No one shall be subjected to arbitrary arrest, detention, or exile.

Article 10

Everyone is entitled in full equality to a fair and public hearing by an independent and impartial tribunal, in the determination of his rights and obligations and of any criminal charge against him.

Article 11

1. Everyone charged with a penal offence has the right to be presumed innocent until proved guilty according to law in a public trial at which he has had all the guarantees necessary for his defence.
2. No one shall be held guilty of any penal offence on account of any act or omission which did not constitute a penal offence,

under national or international law, at the time when it was committed. Nor shall a heavier penalty be imposed than the one that was applicable at the time the penal offence was committed.

Article 12

No one shall be subjected to arbitrary interference with his privacy, family, home, or correspondence, nor to attacks upon his honour and reputation. Everyone has the right to the protection of the law against such interference or attacks.

Article 13

1. Everyone has the right to freedom of movement and residence within the borders of each state.
2. Everyone has the right to leave any country, including his own, and to return to his country.

Article 14

1. Everyone has the right to seek and to enjoy in other countries asylum from persecution.
2. This right may not be invoked in the case of prosecutions genuinely arising from nonpolitical crimes or from acts contrary to the purposes and principles of the United Nations.

Article 15

1. Everyone has the right to a nationality.
2. No one shall be arbitrarily deprived of his nationality nor denied the right to change his nationality.

Article 16

1. Men and women of full age, without any limitation due to race, nationality, or religion, have the right to marry and to found a

family. They are entitled to equal rights as to marriage, during marriage, and at its dissolution.

2. Marriage shall be entered into only with the free and full consent of the intending spouses.
3. The family is the natural and fundamental group unit of society and is entitled to protection by society and the State.

Article 17

1. Everyone has the right to own property alone as well as in association with others.
2. No one shall be arbitrarily deprived of his property.

Article 18

Everyone has the right to freedom of thought, conscience, and religion; this right includes freedom to change his religion or belief, and freedom, either alone or in community with others and in public or private, to manifest his religion or belief in teaching, practice, worship, and observance.

Article 19

Everyone has the right to freedom of opinion and expression; this right includes freedom to hold opinions without interference and to seek, receive, and impart information and ideas through any media and regardless of frontiers.

Article 20

1. Everyone has the right to freedom of peaceful assembly and association.
2. No one may be compelled to belong to an association.

Article 21

1. Everyone has the right to take part in the government of his country, directly or through freely chosen representation.
2. Everyone has the right to equal access to public service in his country.
3. The will of the people shall be the basis of the authority of government; this will shall be expressed in periodic and genuine elections which shall be by universal and equal suffrage and shall be held by secret vote or by equivalent free voting procedures.

Article 22

Everyone, as a member of society, has the right to social security and is entitled to realization, through national effort and international cooperation and in accordance with the organization and resources of each State, of the economic, social, and cultural rights indispensable for his dignity and the free development of his personality.

Article 23

1. Everyone has the right to work, to free choice of employment, to just and favourable conditions of work, and to protection against unemployment.
2. Everyone, without any discrimination, has the right to equal pay for equal work.
3. Everyone who works has the right to just and favourable remuneration ensuring for himself and his family an existence worthy of human dignity and supplemented, if necessary, by other means of social protection.
4. Everyone has the right to form and to join trade unions for the protection of his interests.

Article 24

Everyone has the right to rest and leisure, including reasonable limitation of working hours and periodic holidays with pay.

Article 25

1. Everyone has the right to a standard of living adequate for the health and well-being of himself and of his family, including food, clothing, housing and medical care and necessary social services, and the right to security in the event of unemployment, sickness, disability, widowhood, old age, or other lack of livelihood in circumstances beyond his control.
2. Motherhood and childhood are entitled to special care and assistance. All children, whether born in or out of wedlock, shall enjoy the same social protection.

Article 26

1. Everyone has the right to education. Education shall be free, at least in the elementary and fundamental stages. Elementary education shall be compulsory. Technical and professional education shall be made generally available, and higher education shall be equally accessible to all on the basis of merit.
2. Education shall be directed to the full development of the human personality and to the strengthening of respect for human rights and fundamental freedoms. It shall promote understanding, tolerance, and friendship among all nations, racial, or religious groups, and shall further the activities of the United Nations for the maintenance of peace.
3. Parents have a prior right to choose the kind of education that shall be given to their children.

Article 27

1. Everyone has the right freely to participate in the cultural life of the community, to enjoy the arts, and to share in scientific advancement and its benefits.
2. Everyone has the right to the protection of the moral and material interests resulting from any scientific, literary, or artistic production of which he is the author.

Article 28

Everyone is entitled to a social and international order in which the rights and freedoms set forth in this Declaration can be fully realized.

Article 29

1. Everyone has duties to the community in which alone the free and full development of his personality is possible.
2. In the exercise of his rights and freedoms, everyone shall be subject only to such limitations as are determined by law solely for the purpose of securing due recognition and respect for the rights and freedoms of others and of meeting the just requirements of morality, public order, and the general welfare in a democratic society.
3. These rights and freedoms may in no case be exercised contrary to the purposes and principles of the United Nations.

Article 30

Nothing in this Declaration may be interpreted as implying for any State, group, or person any right to engage in any activity or to perform any act aimed at the destruction of any of the rights and freedoms set forth herein.

Suggested Reading

Brake, T. (1997). *The global leader: Critical factors for creating the world class organization*. Chicago: Irwin Professional.

Brake, T., & Walker, D. M. (1995). *Doing business internationally: The guide to cross-cultural success*. Princeton, NJ: Training Management Corporation.

Dalton, M. A. (1998). *Becoming a more versatile learner*. Greensboro, NC: Center for Creative Leadership.

Dalton, M. A., & Hollenbeck, G. P. (1996). *How to design an effective system for developing managers*. Greensboro, NC: Center for Creative Leadership.

Derr, C. B. (1986). *Managing the new careerists*. San Francisco: Jossey-Bass.

Friedman, T. L. (1999). *The Lexus and the olive tree*. New York: Anchor Books.

Hall, E. T. (1976). *Beyond culture*. New York: Doubleday.

Hay/McBer. (1995). *Mastering global leadership* (A Technical Report). Boston, MA: HayGroup/McBer.

Heifetz, R. A. (1994). *Leadership without easy answers*. Cambridge, MA: Belknap Press of Harvard University Press.

Hofstede, G. (1980). *Culture's consequences: International differences in work-related values*. Thousand Oaks, CA: Sage.

Hofstede, G. (1991). *Cultures and organizations: Software of the mind*. London: McGraw-Hill.

Kanter, R. M. (1995). *World class: Thriving locally in the global economy*. New York: Simon & Schuster.

Kets de Vries, M., & Mead, C. (1992). The development of the global leader within the multinational corporation. In V. Pucik, N. M. Tichy, & C. K. Barnett (Eds.), *Globalizing management: Creating and leading the competitive organization* (pp. 187–205). New York: Wiley.

Kets de Vries, M.F.R., & Florent-Treacy, E. (1999). *The new global leaders: Richard Branson, Percy Barnevik, and David Simon* (1st ed.). San Francisco: Jossey-Bass.

Korn, L. B. (1989, May 22). How the next CEO will be different. *Fortune,* pp. 157–158.

McCauley, C. D., Moxley, R. S., & Van Velsor, E. (Eds.). (1998). *The Center for Creative Leadership handbook of leadership development* (1st ed.). San Francisco: Jossey-Bass and Center for Creative Leadership.

Prince, D. W., & Hoppe, M. H. (2000). *Communicating across cultures.* Greensboro, NC: Center for Creative Leadership.

Rosen, R. H. (2000). *Global literacies: Lessons on business leadership and national cultures: A landmark study of CEOs from twenty-eight countries.* New York: Simon & Schuster.

Schwartz, S. H. (1994). Beyond individualism/collectivism: New cultural dimensions of values. In U. Kim, H. C. Triandis, C. Kagitcibase, S-C Choi, & G. Yoon (Eds.), *Individualism and collectivism: Theory, method and applications* (pp. 85–122). Thousand Oaks, CA: Sage.

Smith, P. B., Dugan, S., & Trompenaars, F. (1996). National culture and the values of organizational employees: A dimensional analysis across forty-three nations. *Journal of Cross-Cultural Psychology, 27,* 231–264.

Triandis, H. C. (1994). *Culture and social behavior.* New York: McGraw-Hill.

Trompenaars, F. (1993). *Riding the waves of culture: Understanding cultural diversity in business.* London: Economist Books.

World Business Council for Sustainable Development Web site. (2001). Available online: http://www.wbcsd.org. (Access date: October 14, 2001.)

References

Adler, N. (1997). *International dimensions of organizational behavior.* Cincinnati, OH: South-Western College Publishing.

Adler, N. J. (1999). Global leadership: Women leaders. In W. H. Mobley, M. J. Gessner, & V. Arnold (Eds.), *Advances in global leadership* (Vol. 1, pp. 49–73). Stamford, CT: JAI Press.

Adler, N. J., & Bartholomew, S. (1992). Managing globally competent people. *Academy of Management Executive, 6*(3), 52–64.

Barrick, M. R., & Mount, M. K. (1991). The Big Five personality dimensions and job performance: A meta-analysis. *Personnel Psychology, 44,* 1–26.

Bartlett, C. A., & Ghoshal, S. (1989). *Managing across borders: The transnational solution.* Boston: Harvard Business School Press.

Bass, B. M. (1997). Does the transactional-transformational leadership paradigm transcend organizational and national boundaries? *American Psychologist, 52*(2), 130–139.

Caux Round Table. (1994). *Principles for business.* Available online: http://www.cauxroundtable.org/ENGLISH.HTM.

Costa, P. T., & McCrae, R. R. (1992). *Revised NEO Personality Inventory and NEO Five-Factor Inventory: Professional manual.* Odessa, FL: PAR.

Dachler, H. P. (1999). A European perspective. In W. H. Mobley, M. J. Gessner, & V. Arnold (Eds.), *Advances in global leadership* (pp. 75–98). Stamford, CT: JAI Press.

Dalton, M. A. (1998). Developing leaders for global roles. In C. D. McCauley, R. S. Moxley, & E. Van Velsor (Eds.), *The Center for*

Creative Leadership handbook of leadership development (1st ed., pp. 379–402). San Francisco: Jossey-Bass and Center for Creative Leadership.

Dalton, M. A., & Rogolsky, S. (1990). *Is that still true? Updates on Key Events Research for women of the 90s.* Greensboro, NC: Center for Creative Leadership.

Den Hartog, D. N., House, R. J., Hanges, P. J., Ruiz-Quintanilla, S. A., & Dorfman, P. W. (1999). Culture specific and cross-culturally generalizable implicit leadership theories: Are attributes of charismatic/transformational leadership universally endorsed? *Leadership Quarterly, 10*(2), 219–256.

Derr, C. B., & Laurent, A. (1989). The internal and external careers: A theoretical and cross-cultural perspective. In M. Arthur, D. T. Hall, & B. S. Lawrence (Eds.), *The handbook of career theory.* Cambridge, England: Cambridge University Press.

Doremus, P. N., Keller, W. W., Pauly, L. W., & Reich, S. (1998). *The myth of the global corporation.* Princeton, NJ: Princeton University Press.

Dorfman, P. (1996). International and cross-cultural leadership. In B. Purnett & O. Shenkar (Eds.), *Handbook for international management research.* Cambridge, MA: Blackwell Business.

Douglas, C. A. (forthcoming). *Lessons of a diverse workforce: A research report.* Greensboro, NC: Center for Creative Leadership.

Feldman, D. C., & Thompson, H. B. (1992). Entry shock, culture shock: Socializing the new breed of global managers. *Human Resource Management, 31*(4), 345–362.

Gardner, H. (1983). *Frames of mind: The theory of multiple intelligences.* New York: Basic Books.

General Assembly of the United Nations. (1948, December 10). *Universal declaration of human rights.* Available online: http://www.un.org/Overview/rights.html.

Goode, E. (2000, August 8). How culture molds habits of thought. *New York Times*, p. F1.

Gregersen, H. B., Morrison, A. J., & Black, J. S. (1998, Fall). Developing leaders for the global frontier. *Sloan Management Review*, pp. 21–32.

Hammer, T. H. (1999). A European perspective. In W. H. Mobley, M. J. Gessner, & V. Arnold (Eds.), *Advances in global leadership* (pp. 99–113). Stamford, CT: JAI Press.

Hill, R. (1992). *We Europeans*. Brussels: Europublications.

Hoppe, M. (1998). Cross-cultural issues in leadership development. In C. D. McCauley, R. S. Moxley, & E. Van Velsor (Eds.), *The Center for Creative Leadership handbook of leadership development* (1st ed., pp. 336–378). San Francisco: Jossey-Bass and Center for Creative Leadership.

Hoppe, M. H. (2000). *The cultural adaptability module*. Greensboro, NC: Center for Creative Leadership.

Howard, P. J., Medina, P. L., & Howard, J. M. (1996). The Big Five Locator—A quick assessment tool for consultants and trainers. In *The 1996 Annual: Volume 1, Training*. San Francisco: Jossey-Bass/Pfeiffer.

Judge, T. A., & Bono, J. E. (2000). Five-Factor model of personality and transformational leadership. *Journal of Applied Psychology, 85*(5), 751–765.

Judge, T. A., Higgins, C. A., Thoresen, C. J., & Barrick, M. R. (1999). The Big Five personality traits, general mental ability, and career success across the life span. *Personnel Psychology, 52*, 621–652.

Kaplan, R. R. (1997). *SKILLSCOPE*. Greensboro, NC: Center for Creative Leadership.

Laurent, A. (1986). The cross-cultural puzzle of international human resource management. *Human Resource Management, 25*(1), 91–102.

LePine, J., Colquitt, J. A., & Erez, A. (2000). Adaptability to changing task contexts: Effects of general cognitive ability, conscientiousness, and openness to experience. *Personnel Psychology, 53*, 563–593.

Lerner, A. J., & Lowe, F. (1959). Why can't the English? On *My fair lady* [Record]. London: Columbia Records.

Leslie, J., Dalton, M., Ernst, C., & Deal, J. (forthcoming). *Managerial effectiveness in a global context: A working model of predictors*. Greensboro, NC: Center for Creative Leadership.

Leslie, J. B., Gryskiewicz, N. D., & Dalton, M. A. (1998). Understanding cultural influences on the 360-degree feedback process. In W. W. Tornow & M. London (Eds.), *Maximizing the value of 360-degree feedback* (pp. 196–216). San Francisco: Jossey-Bass and Center for Creative Leadership.

McCall, M. W., Jr., Lombardo, M. M., & Morrison, A. M. (1988). *The lessons of experience: How successful executives develop on the job*. Lexington, MA: Lexington Books.

McCall, M. W., Jr., Spreitzer, G. M., & Mahoney, J. (1996). *Prospector: Discovering the ability to learn and to lead*. Greensboro, NC: Center for Creative Leadership.

McCauley, C. D., & Brutus, S. (1998). *Management development through job experiences: An annotated bibliography*. Greensboro, NC: Center for Creative Leadership.

McCrae, R. R., & Costa, P. T., Jr. (1997). Personality trait structure as a human universal. *American Psychologist, 52*(5), 509–516.

McDowell, S., & Steed, J. (2000). Fitness for leadership. *Leadership in Action, 19*(6), 6–8.

Miller, S. (2000, December 13). VW starts work on a new model: Profits—Auto maker sets out to please investors. *Wall Street Journal*, pp. A21-A22.

Mintzberg, H. (1973). *The nature of managerial work*. New York: Harper-Collins.

Mintzberg, H. (1990, March-April). Manager's job: Folklore and fact. *Harvard Business Review*, pp. 163–176.

Mintzberg, H. (1994, Fall). Rounding out the manager's job. *Sloan Management Review*, pp. 11–26.

Mitroff, I. I. (1987). *Business not as usual*. San Francisco: Jossey-Bass.

Narang, R., & Devaiah, D. (2000, September 1). *Radical challenges and paradigms of trans-world collaboration*. Paper presented at the HRD Asia 2000 Conference, Singapore.

Onishi, N. (2001, July 29). The bondage of poverty that produces chocolate. *New York Times*, p. 1.

Palmer, J. (1988). *Diversity: Three paradigms*. Unpublished working paper. Cincinnati, OH: Procter & Gamble.

Parker, B. (1996). Evolution and revolution: From international business to globalization. In R. Clegg, C. Hardy, & W. R. Nord (Eds.), *Handbook of organization studies* (pp. 484–506). London: Sage.

PricewaterhouseCoopers. (1999). *Inside the mind of the CEO: The 1999 global CEO survey* (Survey results). New York: PricewaterhouseCoopers.

Ratiu, I. (1983). Thinking internationally—a comparison of how international executives learn. *International Studies of Management and Organization, 13*(1–2), 139–150.

Reich, R. (1991). *The work of nations: Preparing ourselves for twenty-first-century capitalism*. New York: Knopf.

Rhinesmith, S. H. (1993). *A manager's guide to globalization: Six keys to success in a changing world*. Homewood, IL: Business One Irwin.

Roddick, A. (1998). *Body and soul*. New York: Crown.

Ronen, S., & Shenkar, O. (1985). Clustering countries on attitudinal dimensions: A review and synthesis. *Academy of Management Review, 3*, 435–453.

Salgado, J. F. (1997). The five-factor model of personality and job performance in the European Community. *Journal of Applied Psychology, 82*, 30–43.

Segall, M. H., Dasen, P. R., Berry, J. W., & Poortinga, Y. H. (1999). *Human behavior in a global perspective: An introduction to cross-cultural psychology*. Needham Heights, MA: Allyn & Bacon.

Sessa, V. I., Hansen, M. C., Prestridge, S., & Kossler, M. E. (1999). *Geographically dispersed teams: An annotated bibliography*. Greensboro, NC: Center for Creative Leadership.

Simon, P. (1980). *The tongue-tied American: Confronting the foreign language crisis*. New York: Continuum.

Smith, P. B., Peterson, M. F., & Schwartz, S. H. (forthcoming). Cultural values, sources of guidance, and their relevance to managerial behavior: A forty-seven nation study. *Journal of Cross-Cultural Psychology*.

Tagliabue, J. (2001, February 25). At a French factory, culture is a two-way street. *New York Times*, Section 3, p. 4.

Wilson, M. S., Hoppe, M. H., & Sayles, L. R. (1996). *Managing across cultures: A learning framework*. Greensboro, NC: Center for Creative Leadership.

Index

About the Center for Creative Leadership

Founded in 1970, the Center for Creative Leadership® (CCL®) is one of the world's largest institutions focusing on disseminating practical leadership knowledge for individuals and organizations. CCL's mission of advancing the understanding, practice, and development of leadership for the benefit of society worldwide has led to international recognition of its portfolio of programs, assessments, and publications. They are regarded among the best offered by any institution anywhere. The portfolio is supported by CCL's five practice areas—Leadership for Complex Challenges, Leading in the Context of Difference, Individual Leader Development, Sustainable Leadership Capacity, and Team Development.

Funding is derived primarily from tuition, sales of products and publications, royalties, and fees for service. In addition, CCL also seeks grants and donations from foundations, corporations, and individuals in support of its educational mission.

Open-Enrollment Leadership Programs

CCL's open-enrollment leadership programs focus on individuals and may be used within the context of an organization's leadership development efforts. These programs help participants achieve specific developmental goals.

- The *Leadership Development Program*® (LDP), *Foundations of Leadership*, and *The Looking Glass Experience* enable growth through developing personal awareness of one's leadership style and through identifying key areas of strength and weakness.

- *The African-American Leadership Program* and *The Women's Leadership Program* combine personal awareness of one's leadership style with research-based insights to show how leadership is affected by race and gender issues.

- The *Leading Creatively* program helps to understand how business performance and individual effectiveness relate to creativity.

- *Leadership at the Peak* and *Developing the Strategic Leader* use simulations and assessments to gain knowledge about how to lead and inspire change and revitalization.

- *Leadership and High-Performance Teams* shows how to develop and lead teams, turning average performers into a highly effective work group.

- *Coaching for Results* affirms the value of one-on-one developmental assistance, showing how it can be used to enhance individual and organizational effectiveness.

In October 2001, for the second consecutive time, CCL was ranked #1 for Leadership in *BusinessWeek* magazine's Executive Education Special Report. And CCL was the only non-degree business school to appear in *BusinessWeek*'s top 20 providers of non-degree programs for executives. Please visit *www.ccl.org/programs*

Custom-Designed Leadership Development Initiatives

On request, CCL can design and implement a leadership development initiative for your organization, designed specifically to meet its needs. Initiatives vary from redesigned versions of one of CCL's open-enrollment programs to unique events that build an organization from the ground up. Please visit *www.ccl.org/custom*

Coaching

CCL has long understood the importance of honest, insightful, and confidential coaching in developing strong leaders. Our programs are distinct, and all include a reliance on quality assessment; rigorously trained coaches, ethics, and confidentiality; emphasis on the individual's development; and use of best practices throughout. For information on *Follow-on Coaching* (follows leadership programs), *Executive Coaching* (a venue for organizations that want a designed program without the classroom experience), and *Awareness Program for Executive Excellence®* (*APEX*)—for the most senior-level executives), please visit *www.ccl.org/coaching*

Products

CCL pioneered the use of 360-degree assessment and feedback to help individuals, teams, and organizations learn about themselves. Assessments are an effective and necessary starting point for learning, growth, and change. Critical tools in both CCL and clients' development programs, they are also used on a stand-alone basis. CCL can provide facilitation services or train your trainers and facilitators in the use of these resources:

- *360 BY DESIGN*℠, a customizable, Internet-based 360-degree survey with on-line development planning and available support services.
- *Benchmarks®*, CCL's flagship 360-degree assessment tool that focuses on leadership skills and perspectives but also includes insights into potential flaws that can derail a career.
- *Prospector®*, for assessing ability to learn and willingness to take advantage of growth opportunities.

- *SKILLSCOPE®*, for assessing skills necessary for managerial effectiveness.

- *KEYS® to Creativity*, for organizations that want to enhance the environment for creativity and innovation.

Please visit *www.ccl.org/assessments*

Publications

Through its publications, CCL aims to improve the current understanding, practice, and development of leadership by disseminating the latest practical knowledge gained in the course of CCL's research and educational activities. In addition to copublishing books and a magazine with Jossey-Bass, a Wiley company, on a variety of leadership topics, CCL also publishes independently through CCL Press.

Of particular interest to many leaders is the CCL Press *Ideas Into Action* Guidebook series. Geared to the practicing manager, these accessible and concise publications offer proven advice for carrying out a specific developmental task or solving a specific leadership problem. *Ideas Into Action* titles include:

Feedback That Works: How to Build and Deliver Your Message
Keeping Your Career On Track: Twenty Success Strategies
Reaching Your Development Goals
Learning from Life: Turning Life's Lessons into Leadership Experience

Please visit *www.ccl.org/publications*

For more information on CCL's practice areas or special research that may help you in developing solutions for your organization's issues, please call CCL Client Services, (336) 545–2810, e-mail to *info@leaders.ccl.org*, or visit *www.ccl.org*

More About Global Leadership and Leading in the Context of Differences

Leading in the Context of Differences is one of the five practice areas at the Center for Creative Leadership. The work in this area focuses on developing the capacities to lead when the orientations of leaders and those they deal with do not arise from a common set of assumptions. It encompasses the leadership issues of women, African-Americans, and those from different nations and cultures. This book addresses the challenges of the latter group—those who are with organizations that intend to grow globally or in selected regions in the world.

Additional activities that relate to the global aspect of the work of this group that may be of further interest include:

Publications (available at www.ccl.org/publications)

- *Managerial Effectiveness in a Global Context*, Jean Leslie, Maxine Dalton, Chris Ernst, and Jennifer Deal. This report thoroughly documents the research that supported the work of this book (available April 2002).
- *International Success: Selecting, Developing, and Supporting Expatriate Managers*, Meena S. Wilson and Maxine A. Dalton.
- *Communicating Across Cultures*, Don W. Prince and Michael H. Hoppe.
- *Managing Across Cultures: A Learning Framework*, Meena S. Wilson, Michael H. Hoppe, and Leonard Sayles.

Custom Program (call 336-545-2810 for information)

The material presented in this book is available as a two-day custom program specifically designed for global managers. It includes several modules and 360-degree feedback on how to develop the essential managerial capabilities and the pivotal capabilities described in Chapters 2 and 3.

Further Research (contact Maxine Dalton at daltonm@leaders.ccl.org for more information)

The research project currently under way is entitled "Leadership Across Differences: Reconciling Ethnicity, Religion, Gender, and Culture." An international research team has been assembled to look at the role of leaders in organizations where there are groups of people who harbor tension, distrust, and antipathy for other groups in their workplace.